# Your Core Reading Program & Children's Literature

## Effective Strategies for Using the Best of Both

## Diane Barone & Suzette Youngs

■ SCHOLASTIC

New York • Toronto • London • Auckland • Sydney
Mexico City • New Delhi • Hong Kong • Buenos Aires

Cover design: Brian LaRossa

Interior design: LDL Designs

Acquiring Editor: Lois Bridges

Production Editor: Jane Buchbinder

Copy Editor: Shelley Griffin

ISBN-13: 978-0-545-04707-4

ISBN-10: 0-545-04707-2

Copyright © 2008 by Diane Barone and Suzette Youngs

All rights reserved. Published by Scholastic Inc.

Printed in the U.S.A.

1 2 3 4 5 6 7 8 9 10   40   12 11 10 09 08

# $\mathcal{C}$ontents

## CHAPTER 1

# *U*sing the Best of Both: Why a Core Reading Program and Literature-Based Approach Works

*If we had told you then, you might not have gone—and, as you've discovered, so many things are possible just as long as you don't know they're impossible.*

—Norton Juster, *The Phantom Tollbooth*

We chose this quote to begin *Your Core Reading Program & Children's Literature: Effective Strategies for Using the Best of Both* because it offers a literacy curricula for young children that moves beyond real or implied constraints. We believe using a core reading program and children's literature will allow you to experience the science of teaching as well as the art of teaching. We understand the value of reading research that has led to more systematic and explicit instruction to support young children as they become proficient readers and writers (National Reading Panel, 2000), but we also value the art of teaching, which leads to joy for both teachers and students. We have written this book to help you engage your curiosity and creativity as you plan for literacy instruction. We believe that exemplary literacy instruction for young children must be grounded in joyful anticipation of the possibilities—the *what ifs*—of teaching and learning.

Lately, we have listened in on many conversations among teachers and principals that dichotomize core reading programs and literature-based curricula. From these conversations it would appear that there's only one option—either a core reading program or a literature-based curricula. We believe this view is limiting and inaccurate, as we see teachers successfully using both. When both approaches are integrated in the classroom, students benefit from interdisciplinary learning experiences that engage them in rich content as they gain insights into literature and literacy.

We understand that in many schools and districts, there is an expectation to use a core reading program for a 90-minute uninterrupted block of instruction. This is especially true for schools that have received Reading First grants or qualify for Title I funds. But teaching just one core program can limit the way you teach your students to read and write. Even when a core reading program is mandated, the rest of the day offers many opportunities to teach reading and writing in other ways. You might respond to this suggestion with something like "Are you kidding? We have no time to do anything else!" We understand the limitations of time and the pressures to provide instruction in all curricular areas. Our response is to offer practical ways that you can use literacy—reading, writing, speaking, and listening—as a vehicle to deepen your students' understanding and motivation to read and write, and to learn other content areas as they develop these abilities.

This chapter begins with a discussion of effective literacy practices for primary children. It then moves to a discussion of the pros and cons of using core reading programs and literature-based curricula. From this foundation, we consider the pragmatic issues centered on using both in primary classrooms.

# Exemplary Literacy Instruction

Exemplary literacy instruction occurs in classrooms where a literate environment has been created even before the students arrive. When they first enter the classroom, the students are enfolded into an environment that supports literacy. They notice a classroom library with multiple books, with many organized into tubs related to themes or levels. There are books at a table related to a unit of study, such as books written by a single author or books about a particular topic, such as plants. Students' names are featured near the entry to the room and near their cubbies. Labels point out other areas of the room as well, such as the meeting circle and the teacher's desk. A writing center beckons with paper, writing utensils, and computers. On the walls children see the alphabet and sound cards. A word wall, which features the alphabet with space for words, suggests the word work in which the children will engage throughout the year. A bulletin board with open space awaits the student work that will soon be displayed. Additionally, the students may notice a journal on their desk or table space with a pencil for writing (Barone, Mallette, & Xu, 2005; Pressley, Rankin, & Yokoi, 1996; Pressley, 2006a).

The National Reading Report findings (2000) and other research evidence provide guidance for literacy instruction. Research has shown the need for systematic phonological awareness, phonemic awareness, and phonics instruction. In addition to this instruction to help children learn the alphabetic code, instruction in comprehension, fluency, and vocabulary are critical to developing young readers and writers. Pressley et al. (1996) noted that teachers with high student achievement provided multiple opportunities in a single day for children to be actively engaged in stories and informational text. As teachers read, they quickly helped children understand an unfamiliar word and stopped to model their thinking about the selection, thus making the comprehension process accessible to young children. Teachers encouraged children to share thoughts and questions with other students, and to contribute to whole-class discussion to keep them engaged in the comprehension process.

Pressley et al.'s exploration of exemplary first-grade teachers found that the teachers continuously modeled comprehension and writing strategies. They reorganized students into multiple groupings to maximize learning, such as forming a group for targeted reteaching of a skill or strategy. This group worked together until children acquired the skill or strategy. Other groupings included book clubs and writing partnerships. Most importantly, exemplary first-grade teachers balanced instruction in word-level knowledge with meaning making. That is, they supported students in their knowledge of letters, letters matched to sounds, and, finally, decoding. Students had opportunities to practice their tentative knowledge of decoding through reading decodable texts. These exemplary teachers did not limit children, however, to just letter and word knowledge. They provided opportunities to engage with narrative and informational text, with teacher support when necessary, so that children understood the importance of meaning making while reading. To support meaning making, teachers read to children, sharing important words and ideas so that children were nudged toward more complex ways of understanding texts.

A similar study conducted by Taylor, Pearson, Clark, and Walpole (1999) explored exemplary teachers in first, second, and third grades with children in high-poverty schools. They noted that in addition to focusing on word- and meaning-level elements of text, students who spent more time in small-group instruction had higher achievement. In these groups, teachers more carefully targeted instruction to the variable learning needs of students. Not surprisingly, these teachers effectively used informal assessments to guide instruction and decision making about the composition of students in each group.

Taylor et al.'s study also reported that effective literacy teachers spent more time teaching reading than did other teachers. Typically they engaged students in reading activities for approximately 134 minutes daily. They also provided about a half hour each day for students to read independently. Clearly, exemplary literacy teachers have abundant energy that they use to guide and enhance student learning.

In addition to focusing on reading at word and text level, exemplary teachers understand the importance of writing both to develop and expand reading competency and to communicate (Pressley, 2006b). Even though the National Reading Panel report did not focus on writing, exemplary teachers have not excluded it from a central place in their literacy curricula. They model writing, support children's writing by scaffolding (interactive writing), have children write independently in learning logs and journals, and support students as they write longer texts with revision and editing. Writing is an important daily literacy activity.

To sum up the research on young children's future literacy achievement, Pressley (2006b) and Snow, Burns, and Griffin (1998) indicate that the following areas of instruction and learning are significant.

- **Understanding and using the alphabetic principle.** Children have acquired phonological and phonemic knowledge. They can read and represent words using letter-sound knowledge. They are becoming fluent as they read grade-level material.
- **Understanding print functions.** Children understand why they read and write, and they can express themselves orally and in writing.
- **Vocabulary and knowledge.** Children have developed vocabulary knowledge to support their comprehension. Children also have developed the necessary background knowledge to understand the concepts and ideas shared in text. This also includes knowledge of various genres.
- **Motivation.** Children enjoy reading and writing and readily engage in these activities.

Overall, at the end of the primary grades, children have acquired sufficient word knowledge to read and write most single-syllable words accurately. They are relatively fluent (40 words per minute end of first grade, 90 words per minute at end of second, and 110 words per minute end of third [Good, Simmons, & Kame'enui, 2002]), and they can simultaneously read and comprehend narrative and informational text. These are baseline benchmarks used to determine the ease or difficulty of young children's present and future literacy development.

Moreover, students read, write, speak, and listen with competence, ease, and pleasure. As Gambrell, Malloy, and Mazzoni (2007) describe, "Comprehensive literacy instruction emphasizes the personal, intellectual, and social nature of literacy learning, and supports the notion that students learn new meanings in response to new experiences rather than simply learning what others have created" (p. 14). This description fits the blending of core reading programs and literature-based curricula described throughout this book.

# Core Reading Programs

Core reading programs are not new to elementary schools, and not surprisingly educators both support and criticize such programs (Lapp, Fisher, Flood, Goss-Moore, & Moore, 2002). According to Hoffman et al. (1998), the McGuffey Readers, first published in the 1830s, are considered the first basal reading series. From this early beginning, basals have undergone a multitude of configurations. The earliest basals in the 1930s relied on controlled vocabulary. Later, basals moved away from a narrow focus on control and began to include phonics and sight-word instruction (Popp, 1975). In the 1970s the focus shifted to basals that were more skills-based, with accompanying workbooks for practice. These basals also included an assessment strand for teachers. Not surprisingly, critics challenged the skills-based organization, and the importance of quality literature emerged (Hoffman et al., 1998). During the late 1980s and 1990s, basals were renamed literature-based anthologies. From these traditions came the current evolution of the basal in core reading programs that represent elements from all previous basal cycles. Despite criticism, core reading programs are still the most commonly used materials to teach children to read (Fawson & Reutzel, 2000), perhaps because of their continuous changes to meet current student and teacher needs. Principals tend to favor core reading programs because they come as complete packages, so support materials, such as assessments, need not be purchased (Lapp et al., 2002).

Most current core reading programs provide materials and instruction for all of the language arts, including reading, writing, listening, and speaking, with units organized by theme for students in kindergarten through eighth grade. The programs consist of teachers' and students' editions of the literature anthologies, leveled text for differentiated instruction, phonics decodable texts, assessments, workbooks, and other ancillary materials including Internet support. In fact, in schools where we have worked, it often takes teachers a few years to realize all of the support materials provided in a core reading program. These programs are organized so that each day children participate in whole-class and small-group instruction; differentiation is a key component. Most programs also provide materials for reteaching struggling students and support materials for children new to English.

Beyond principals' desires to purchase an entire program to meet the literacy learning needs of children, there are other compelling reasons to use a core reading program. The primary reason is continuity within a school, district, and even a state in the presentation of skills and strategies to students. A core reading program provides a broad, comprehensive view of reading that supports continuity of instruction within a grade level and across grade levels. While not diminishing the individual talents of teachers, a core reading program assures that a literacy curriculum is more than a series of individual instructional events provided by teachers.

Second, a core reading program provides a framework for teachers who move in and out of a school and may not have been privy to the all-school professional development from the previous year. This situation is more common in schools with high-poverty youngsters, and often results in a fractured literacy curriculum. When the literacy curriculum is based solely on individual decision making, teachers may struggle to design their literacy curriculum, particularly if they are brand new. Through the use of a core program, teachers, even brand-new ones, have sufficient guidance and materials to provide comprehensive reading instruction to students at a variety of reading levels from the first days of school.

Third, the use of a core reading program provides consistency for students who are highly transient. When students move from one school to another in a district, they will see similar word support on the walls of the room, similar structures used in teaching (whole-class and small-group), and opportunities to easily build on previous knowledge gained in other classrooms. They do not have to participate in a guessing game to determine what is expected in the literacy curriculum. Rather, they can focus attention on literacy learning and adjusting to a new teacher and new fellow students.

Finally, using a core program provides opportunities for collaborating on content and activities. You can look across a grade level to determine student strengths and needs as you share similar content and assessments with other teachers. And you can utilize your paraprofessionals and other teacher support to preteach or reteach important skills, strategies, or concepts. For instance, if there is difficult vocabulary in a particular story in the core anthology, the paraprofessional can meet with students who are struggling and preteach this vocabulary so that these students can actively participate in the whole-class lesson.

Detractors of core reading programs most often cite lack of teacher freedom in determining what is best to teach students (Hoffman et al., 1998; Hudak-Huelbig, Keyes, McClure, & Stellingwerf, 1991). Other criticism suggests that schools adopt core programs because teachers lack essential teaching skills. Pressley (2006b) wrote: "Teachers who use published reading materials or teach skills are being de-skilled themselves" (p. 432). He later argued that this made no sense, as many accomplished teachers rely on core materials and then tailor their use of them to the students in their classes.

Some argue that core reading programs do not motivate students to read (Wepner, Strickland, & Feeley, 2002). Critics state that the use of core reading programs limits children's ability to engage with quality literature. Finally, critics argue that textbooks (core reading programs) and the text selections within are chosen by others for children. The texts in these collections are linked to activity pages, and the focus is on skills rather than on an appreciation and understanding of quality children's literature (Peterson & Eeds, 2007).

## Literature-Based Literacy Curricula

A literature-based literacy curriculum is also not new to elementary classrooms. Smith (1979) encouraged teachers to move beyond a focus on phonics and engage children in comprehension through the reading of quality literature. Goodman (1986), building on Smith's work, suggested that learning to read entails informed predictions about the meaning of the text. The reader draws from a variety of psycholinguistic cues—graphophonic, syntactic, semantic, and pragmatic. Goodman's work led teachers away from word-level learning and shifted to children's literature as a basis for instruction. Smith's and Goodman's combined work led to what became known as whole language (Weaver, 2002), in which teachers created their own literacy curriculum using children's literature and leveled texts for independent reading. Teachers were highly supportive of this freedom to develop a literacy curriculum that best met the needs of their students. Schools saw an increase in the purchases of children's books and leveled text support. They witnessed a decrease in anything having to do with phonics instruction, such as sound cards or phonics workbooks.

Teachers often organized their literature-based curricula around a theme, which then determined the topics of books they selected for class sharing. For instance, if the theme was exploration, teachers selected books that focused on explorations, such as science or social studies lessons or explorations conducted by characters in children's books. Young children might experience, for example, the simple exploration the main character in *Spot's First Walk* (Hill, 2004) has when he leaves his mother and explores his neighborhood. Teachers also found leveled text that supported the theme as well. In some schools, we saw teachers organize a whole year's curriculum around a theme, so they would filter an investigation of all subject areas through a theme such as exploration.

In other classrooms, teachers organized themes that lasted about a month before they changed to another theme. When developing themes, teachers often used an organizational structure similar to that shared in Figure 1.1. From this simple web, teachers elaborated on children's books, outlined their reading and writing instruction and activities, listed the content knowledge to be learned, and identified the connections among all.

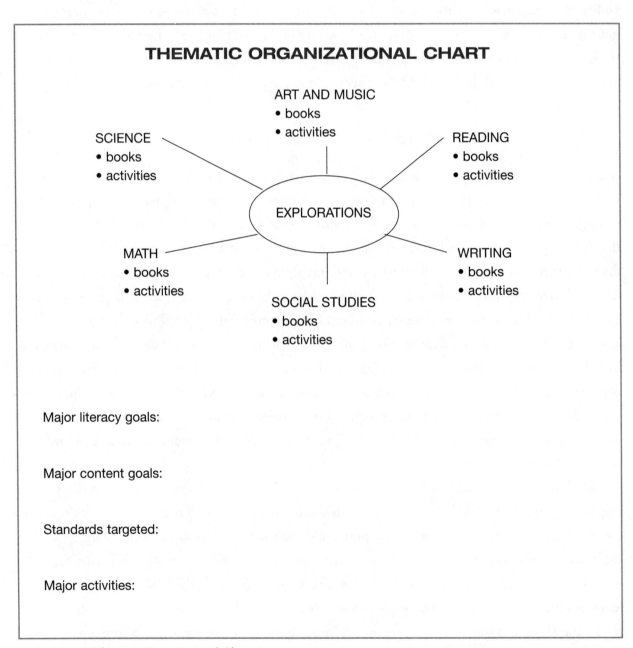

FIGURE 1.1: Thematic Organizational Chart

Pressley (2006b) identifies the strengths of using literature-based curricula to teach children to read. First, children engage in literate behaviors as they learn to read and write (Morrow, 1991). Second, children better understand the structure of various genres as they read high-quality literature and engage in writing activities (Cochran-Smith, 1984). A third strength is the growth of children's vocabulary and world knowledge (Elley, 1989).

Dahl and Freppon's widely known study (1995) is frequently cited as support for more holistic literacy instruction. They compared kindergarten and first-grade students in whole-language and skills-based classrooms and discovered that primary children in the whole-language classes:

- Applied phonics knowledge in writing through the use of approximations and, when reading, corrected errors where meaning was compromised
- Provided more sophisticated oral responses to literature
- Viewed themselves as readers and writers
- Were more engaged with reading and writing activities
- Understood the language of written stories
- Used a variety of strategies to decode an unfamiliar word in text
- Better understood that reading was about gaining meaning

The one concern that arose from this study was that students in the whole-language classrooms typically relied more on picture and semantic cues when encountering an unknown word. Their difficulty with decoding an unknown word through the use of sound-symbol or pattern knowledge was viewed as a challenge for future reading success.

Overall, literature-based curricula offer these numerous strengths.

- Through engagement with children's literature, there are multiple opportunities to talk about text, and student talk is linked to student learning (Nystrand, 1997). This talk also provides opportunities for children to explore comprehension literally, inferentially, and critically (Anstey & Bull, 2006).
- Literature-based curricula allow for extended time for children to engage with text during scaffolded instruction with teachers and independent reading. This additional time spent reading supports students' literacy learning (Peterson & Eeds, 2007; Taylor & Pearson, 2002).
- Providing children with access to children's books increases their motivation to read, and motivation and time spent reading is linked with student achievement (Pressley, Allington, Wharton-McDonald, Block, & Morrow, 2001).

- Literature-based curricula allow children to develop a deep understanding of a topic or theme through multiple exposures to this content in books, discussions, and activities. These long-term investigations of a topic or theme are beneficial to all children: English language learners and special education students come to understand the vocabulary and topic in ways that a single exposure cannot accomplish and grade-level and accelerated students have opportunities to go deeper into a topic and develop more sophisticated understanding.

On the other hand, educators will find three major arguments against the use of literature-based curricula as the sole organizational strategy. First, teachers may not provide a literacy curriculum that targets all of the essential elements of literacy. For instance, they may focus on comprehension over phonics instruction. Second, there is no guaranteed systematic literacy curriculum within a grade or across grades. Teachers may or may not work with other teachers to assure a systematic and consistent instruction of literacy skills and strategies. As a result, children may develop strengths in one area, but not in others. For instance, we have seen teachers prize reading instruction and minimize writing instruction. As children move through a school, they may experience difficulty with writing because they have not had the opportunity to express themselves consistently through writing. Finally, literature-based teachers are often criticized for not paying enough attention to the explicit teaching of word-level skills (Pressley, 2006b).

## Why It Is Important to Use Both

We believe that it is beneficial to student learning to use both core reading programs and literature-based curricula. Through the simultaneous use of both, students receive systematic instruction in skills and strategies, and they have sufficient time to participate in extended reading and writing activities to support decoding, fluency, comprehension, vocabulary, writing, and motivation. Further, by working collaboratively across grade levels and using both, you can provide students with a complete literacy curriculum that is systematic, explicit, and rich in opportunities for individual teacher decision making to support students' literacy achievement. Such a program guarantees that students receive instruction and practice in all the key elements of reading and numerous writing opportunities where there are no missing aspects (e.g., limited vocabulary instruction) or redundant instruction (e.g., reteaching short-vowel sounds in multiple years) (Bean, 2002).

Moreover, we have seen that as teachers integrate core reading programs and literature-based curricula into their classrooms, the result is both exemplary teaching and high student literacy achievement. From the work of Gambrell and Mazzoni (1999), the National Reading Panel (2000), Pressley (2006b), Pressley et al. (2001), and Snow et al. (1998), we note the following components present in classrooms of exemplary literacy teachers.

## General Practices

- Wide variety of teaching strategies that result in student engagement
- High expectations and respect for all students
- Differentiated instruction to meet the learning strengths and needs of students
- Consistent feedback to students about their learning
- Varied well-organized patterns to support student learning
- Assessment that results in changes in instruction
- Parents as an integral part of the classroom
- Teacher-motivated professional development and peer collaboration

## Literacy Practices

- Literacy-rich classroom environment
- Sequential reading curriculum that targets phonological awareness, phonics, fluency, comprehension, and vocabulary
- Variety of reading materials, including quality children's literature
- Support at grade level, above grade level, and for struggling students through differentiation of instruction and interventions
- Uninterrupted reading block of at least 90 minutes; additionally, reading and writing integrated throughout the day
- Additional blocks of time for writing instruction and independent reading throughout the day

These characteristics are important to student learning, and they can only be achieved when students have more than a core reading program or a literature-based reading program. We believe that students need both. The first questions posed when considering the use of both core reading programs and literature-based curricula are when and how—big questions that must be answered for teacher success. We tackle the *when* first and then the *how*. In Chapter Five, we offer additional recommendations to make the use of both easier for primary teachers.

## When

We recommend that schools or grade-level teams work together on schedules that support both literacy curricula and other content areas as well. On pages 17 and 18 are two possible schedules for primary classrooms. We offer these as a point of reflection as schools work to create their own schedules to best meet the learning needs of their students. Moreover, even though we set aside blocks of time for instruction, reading, writing, and thinking permeate the whole school day.

As you block out instructional times, you may also want to consider the availability of support personnel. In our experience, principals work with

Mrs. Brown with Anthony, Michael, and Micah at Vanderburg Elementary School in Clark County, Nevada.

first-, second-, and third-grade teachers to make sure that their intervention blocks do not overlap. By staggering these blocks, support personnel are available to provide small-group intervention instruction for students at each grade level.

## How

### Standards Documents

The *how* begins with a school district's or state's language arts standards. No matter how literacy instruction is configured, the standards must be the first consideration in planning for instruction. Most state standards are available on the district and/or state department of education Web sites. In some states, like Texas or California, publishers identify the state standards right in the core reading program as these states typically adopt a core reading program for the entire state. For other states, teachers and/or school districts identify the standards that are addressed within their core reading program and literature-based curriculum.

| SCHEDULE A | | |
|---|---|---|
| 8:30–8:45 | Opening | Children get settled. Teachers may have books for them to read at their desks or journals for writing. This is a great time for rereading and/or journal writing. |
| 8:45–10:15 | Core Reading Program | Teachers begin with whole-class activities and then move to small differentiated groups for guided reading. |
| 10:15–10:45 | Reading Interventions | Teachers within a grade level share children for targeted intervention support. Several teachers and support personnel work with struggling readers; other teachers work with grade-level or above students. |
| 10:45–11:00 | Recess | |
| 11:00–11:30 | Writing Block | Children engage in process writing activities. |
| 11:30–12:00 | Lunch Break | |
| 12:00–1:00 | Math Block | Teachers engage students in whole-class and small-group math instruction and activities. |
| 1:00–2:00 | Literature-Based Curricula | Teachers engage students in literature-based curricula based on theme extension from core reading program. |
| 2:00–2:45 | Science or Social Studies | Instruction is varied. On some days students explore science concepts and on other days or weeks social studies concepts. |
| 2:00–2:30 or 2:30–3:00 | Specials: Art, Music, PE | These classes occur on various schedules in primary classes. On the days that specials are scheduled, social studies or science may be reduced to a 15-minute block. However, social studies and science are also explored during the core reading block and the literature-based curricula block. |
| 2:45–3:00 | Closing | |

| SCHEDULE B | | |
|---|---|---|
| 8:30–8:45 | Opening | Children settle into classroom. They may read or write as a beginning to the day. This is a great time for rereading and/or journal writing. |
| 8:45–10:15 | Core Reading Block | Teachers begin with whole-class activities and then move to small, differentiated groups for guided reading. |
| 10:15–10:30 | Recess | |
| 10:30–11:30 | Math Block | Teachers engage students in whole-class and small-group math instruction and activities. |
| 11:30–12:00 | Writing Block | Children engage in process writing activities. |
| 12:00–12:30 | Lunch Break | |
| 12:30–1:30 | Literature-Based Curricula | Teachers engage students in literature-based curricula based on theme extension from core reading program. |
| 1:30–2:00 | Reading Interventions | Teachers within a grade level share children for targeted intervention support. Several teachers and support personnel work with struggling readers; other teachers work with grade-level or advanced students. |
| 2:00–2:45 | Science or Social Studies | Instruction is varied. Some days students explore science concepts and on other days or weeks social studies concepts. |
| 2:00–2:30 or 2:30–3:00 | Specials: Art, Music, PE | These classes occur on various schedules in primary classes. On the days that specials are scheduled, social studies or science may be reduced to a 15-minute block. However, social studies and science are also explored during the core reading block and the literature-based curricula block. |
| 2:45–3:00 | Closing | |

Once you are clear on the standards you need to address, you can consider your reading and writing curricula and determine where it is sufficient and where it needs shoring up. This is an activity best done with a group of grade-level teachers. The good news is that once this work is completed for a grade level, it does not need repeating until standards are revised or a new core reading program is adopted.

## Choices in the Core Reading Program

Each theme, week's lessons, and daily lessons in a core program offer more suggestions for instruction and practice than anyone could use. Whew! No need to panic over the multitude of activities and lesson expectations—publishers always provide more. These suggestions are there to meet the varied needs of students within a class. Core reading programs also provide a surplus of materials to use for small-group reading and independent work. Once again, we suggest that you refer to your state's standards while also considering your students' needs when choosing which instructional strategies and activities to incorporate into the classroom. Typically, there is also a major goal for each lesson; these are useful in deciding what to teach and what to cut. The directions in core reading programs also suggest that teachers pay special attention to skills or strategies that are assessed at the end of each theme. These targeted skills help with decision making as well.

As we visit and work in schools, we notice that in rooms where students have the highest achievement data, in addition to quality teaching, teachers rely on reading and writing for independent work and minimize the use of worksheets. During independent work, students often have a bag or tub of books at their independent level for rereading. They may be expected to write a response about a book they read independently or in their small-group instruction. Often this response ties to comprehension strategies that were taught, such as interpreting the actions of a character or understanding the importance of the setting to a particular story. And frequently, students are engaged in word work in which they search in their books for words that fit a particular pattern and then record these words in word study notebooks. For example, they may be asked to find words that have the *oo* in them, as in *look*. As they are reading, they note any words that have this pattern and record them. On a subsequent day, they may be asked to find other words with *oo* in them that make a sound as in the word *cool*. Then children can compare the two sounds of *oo*. These kinds of activities are repeated daily so that even when students are not working directly with their teacher they are engaged in authentic reading and writing tasks.

Once you are confident you are meeting the learning needs of students and addressing standards, you can choose a particularly interesting piece of text from the core anthology to use as a benchmark text for literature-based curricula. In this way, connections are made between the two major literacy blocks during a day. In following chapters, we model this practice. Importantly, when selecting the benchmark text, be sure that it is rich enough to support other learning and that it offers numerous opportunities for exploration. Following are some guidelines for the selection of a benchmark text.

- Choose a text that is regarded as quality children's literature.
- Select, throughout the year, a wide variety of text genres, such as narrative, biography, informational, persuasive, and poetry.
- Sample the work of featured illustrators or authors.
- Choose a text that supports important themes for students to explore.
- Find text that connects easily to science or social studies topics.

Consider the important strategies that are emphasized with this text so that time can be provided for practice during the literature-based curriculum portion of the day. For example, if the comprehension strategy is prediction, you might then focus on this strategy in other reading events.

## Literature-Based Curriculum Choices

This is an area where there's lots of leeway in selecting texts and activities. Once you have made a decision on the choice of a benchmark text, gather all the materials that might be appropriate. You might begin with your personal library of books or you could visit the school or city library to find other books to support your theme. Following the collection of books, you may explore Internet sites to support your study. Then comes the creative part: working with grade-level colleagues to determine appropriate activities and learning goals for this portion of the literacy curriculum. During this brainstorming session, you keep in mind all the various areas of literacy, such as comprehension, fluency, vocabulary, writing, genre study, author and/or illustrator study, and so on. We expect that this process will result in more activities and ideas than can be accomplished in a week or month. Then, as with the core program, you can just whittle these to the most important activities to support student learning. While this initial planning may seem overwhelming—and it will be if this is the first time you've participated in this thinking—each successive unit or theme will be easier to accomplish and the time demands will diminish. Moreover, by extending these initial ideas into future units, you'll have a groundwork to build on in the coming years.

## Assessment

Core programs provide many opportunities for assessment of student learning to monitor students' progress throughout an academic year. Literature-based curricula do not come with pre-made assessments. As teachers, you are expected to determine the appropriate assessments for this learning. There are many paths you can take with assessment. The core reading program assessments will help track student growth in literacy skills and strategies. By building on these assessments, you could create rubrics for major activities conducted during the literature-based curriculum block. For instance, if students are writing a report, you might develop a rubric to assess the report. As a result of the rubric, you and your students will be clear about what is expected in terms of process, content, and form. You can also support your students with assessment portfolios where work is collected to support content knowledge or process experiences (Barone & Taylor, 2007).

We acknowledge that using both core reading programs and literature-based curricula is a challenge, but it is a challenge that supports an effective school-wide literacy program. A consistent core reading program supports the need for uniformity in instruction across grades and throughout a school that results in enhanced student learning. A literature-based curriculum supports extending student learning and allows teachers and students more choice in texts and activities. Integrating both provides for the direct, explicit instruction that students need to learn some literacy content and offers opportunities for extensive reading and writing experiences that are necessary to develop competent and motivated readers and writers.

The following chapters provide examples of what this instruction might consist of in first, second, and third grades. We have chosen benchmark texts from several core reading programs. From this foundation, we developed many other literacy activities to support students in learning to read and write. We think that these examples provide the scaffolding for your own instruction to better meet the learning needs of students and to more fully engage them in learning.

# CHAPTER 2

# *F*irst-Grade Possibilities

*I*n many classrooms today teachers are designing and implementing literacy experiences
that encourage students to investigate themes and topics that are not constrained by
curricular boundaries.

—Linda Kucan, Diane Lapp, James Flood, and Douglas Fisher, *Best Practices in Literacy Instruction*

Our view into first grade considers both the 90-minute literacy block organized through a core reading program and extended children's literature activities. We offer an overview of the literacy expectations for a single, core reading selection that would be targeted during the block. Then we expand on these expectations and share literacy possibilities that best fit the needs of students. By reflecting on those activities, you'll be able to imagine how you might bring them into your own literacy curricula. While we have provided numerous activities, we know that you will select those that match your overarching goals, such as comprehension or vocabulary. For instance, in one reading response activity students build comparison charts—not just as an activity to keep busy, but for the larger purpose of deepening informational-text comprehension.

## The Core Reading Program

For our first-grade selection, we have chosen an informational text, *Tadpole to Frog* (Robinson) from the theme Take a Closer Look from the Scott Foresman first-grade core reading program (2004). This eight-page selection describes the life cycle of a frog through the use of photos and charts. It begins with a display of water and eggs, followed by a photo of a tadpole with legs. The next two pages describe the growth of the tadpole, showing his shrinking tail and increased size of body. The following two pages show a frog jumping and include the line, "We like to see tadpoles turn into frogs!" (p. 162). The next page asks questions about where the frog might go and brings to text the rhyming words of *frog* and *log*. The last page features a circular chart with picture support of the frog life cycle.

We chose this text because it is informational, and we believe that bringing extended experiences with informational text to the primary grades is important. Moreover, the author has written numerous other informational texts that appeal to young readers and they are readily available.

The following is a list of the curricular expectations for students based on this informational text selection.

## Comprehension

- Identify why the author wrote the selection; discover that her purpose is to inform
- Use context clues to gain the meaning of words to support comprehension
- Practice prediction to gain meaning
- Identify the sequence of events (a frog's life cycle), thus supporting literal comprehension
- Draw conclusions
- Use the illustrations to support comprehension
- Practice critical thinking through comparing this text selection to a narrative one from the anthology about frogs
- Identify the genre of informational text

## Word Knowledge
### Vocabulary
- Become familiar with these words: *tadpole, body, turn, plump, he's, soon,* and *some*
### Phonics
- Practice the short-vowel sounds of *o, a,* and *i*
- Observe the rhyming words in the text
- Review final *x*
### Word Structure
- Practice with *s* plurals

## Fluency
- Reread the text and/or listen to it on CD and follow along with the text

## Writing
- Write telling sentences
- Participate in modeled writing of a poem
- Engage in reader response prompts such as "Were you surprised by the way the tadpole grew?" (p. 168)

- Respond to various journal prompts such as *Write about a tadpole turning into a frog*
- Practice test preparation questions that follow the selection, such as *Write about each stage of your life* or respond to "Why do you think the tadpole's tail becomes shorter?" (p. 168)
- Create a frog poster with facts about frogs on it

This single selection generated many specific goals for learning. Some are simple like the short-vowel work and review practice. The comprehension activities are multiple and help students understand the life cycle of a frog. And the publisher has offered numerous ways for students to engage in writing related to this text selection.

Leveled texts can support all instructional activities and strategies that are expected of the whole class, and this program also offers opportunities for differentiated small-group practice and extension of the strategies and skills. Just as we offer suggestions for extended literacy curricula, we also recommend that you target the most important strategies and skills taught through this one selection rather than superficially teaching them all. In addition to targeting instruction, you'll also need to select, if any, the most appropriate practice worksheets for students as the program offers more than any one child should be expected to complete. When considering many of the suggestions from the core program and those we offer to extend the program, you may want to avoid worksheets completely and offer students many opportunities to read and write for independent practice.

# The Extended Literacy Curriculum

We believe that informational text selections like *Tadpole to Frog* afford numerous ways to extend and deepen literacy curricula and also to build bridges to science curricula. In this section, we provide multiple ways—more than any one teacher could use—to explore this text. Our hope is that these literacy extensions will inspire you to create other possibilities for literacy learning. We have grouped books under certain categories for ease of presentation, but most of these books simultaneously serve to extend vocabulary and stir writing ideas.

## Reading Connections

We selected numerous books for making reading connections and as extensions of the core reading selection. These books vary in content, structure of text, and difficulty level. We believe that a multitude of books are necessary for reaching each child, as each will have his or her own likes and dislikes. Keep in mind that these are not the only books you might select; a variety of books is what is important.

## Fiction

**Stories About Frogs.** When we selected *Tadpole to Frog* from the core reading program, we had no idea how many narrative books about frogs were available, and appropriate to young readers. We found two series of books about frogs. The Froggy series (London) has more than 15 titles. In *Froggy Goes to School* (London, 1996), Froggy dreams about showing up for his first day of school wearing his underwear. Thankfully, he wakes up to find this is a dream, and he has a successful first day. Children will enjoy reading Froggy stories, becoming more fluent readers as they make their way through the series. The plots in these books are straightforward and allow students to become more practiced as readers. Plus, they will enjoy the multiple silly adventures of Froggy. Another similar series is Frog and Toad (Lobel). Like the Froggy books, Frog and Toad offer numerous opportunities for rereading an enjoyable text, and these stories also follow simple plots so children can get practice and enjoy reading at the same time.

We came up with two simple extensions to these books that will support students' comprehension. First, have children create a chart with facts about Froggy. Children should be able to easily find the facts, most of which are written literally in the text. They can also infer information, such as that Froggy was worried about school because of his dream about being late. Figure 2.1 shows the facts from *Froggy Goes to School.*

Frog and Toad books lend themselves to a more complex chart. Because both Frog and Toad are dominant characters, children can build comparison lists. For instance, in *Days With Frog and Toad* (Lobel, 1979), we learn that Toad is sloppy and likes to procrastinate. These characteristics can be added to Toad's list. Plus while the word *procrastination* never appears in the text, young children would love to learn this word and practice using it throughout the day. Frog, on the other hand, is neat or fastidious and organized, so students can directly compare these traits and enjoy the more sophisticated vocabulary. This more complex chart helps students understand comparisons and could result in a comparative writing piece or a diamante poem. (See Writing Connections in this chapter.)

### FACTS ABOUT FROGGY

1. He wants to go to school. He is worried when he thinks he has missed the bus.
2. He dreams about school and he is worried.
3. His name is the first word he learns to read.
4. He likes his first day of school. He tells his parents all about it.

FIGURE 2.1: Facts About Froggy

Other narratives about frogs include the following.

*Jump, Frog, Jump!* (Kalan, 1981). This book is repetitive, with an additional line added on each subsequent page, and allows student participation with the repetition of the phrase "jump, frog, jump." It also models questions that are answered with the same sentence over and over. The text, for the most part, is not easily accessible for young readers without support from a teacher or more accomplished reader.

*The Icky Sticky Frog* (Bentley, 2000). *The Icky Sticky Frog* is similar to *Jump, Frog, Jump!* in that it allows children to easily join in. On almost every page there is a large word like *WOOP!* or *SLURP!* which children enjoy reading with their teacher. Throughout the books Frog uses his tongue to capture creatures until he is finally captured by a fish. This book is simpler in text structure and young children will be able to read it, although at first they will most likely rely on memorization. The sticky tongue hanging out on the cover will certainly invite students in.

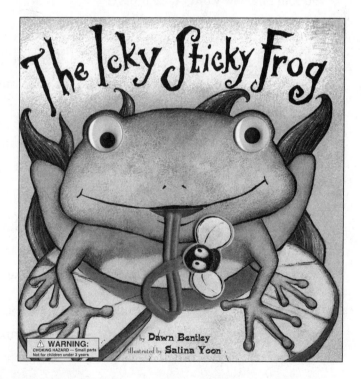

*Fat Frogs on a Skinny Log* (Riches, 2000). This book appears to be a simple counting book with only frogs being counted. However, on each page there are adjectives beginning with the letter *s*, which also grow in number. So, for instance, on the fifth page it says, "Five fat frogs sat on a skinny, slippery, slimy, slithery, sludgy log." On each page, one more frog joins the others on the log until eventually they fall into the water. Children will enjoy reading and rereading all of the *s* adjectives that are added on each page. A good way to extend word knowledge is by having students pay attention to the meaning of the adjectives in addition to their pronunciation. Students would also enjoy creating their own model of this book with adjectives that begin with other letters. The task would not be too difficult as they are only adding one new word on each page.

*One Frog Sang* (Parenteau, 2007). Here's another counting book, but in this one each frog is added to form a symphony through his or her particular sound. For example, two frogs sing "preep, preep." When a car comes by all the frogs are silent for a short time and then they begin their grunts, croaks, and chirps once again.

*Stick* (Breen, 2007). This is a story of a frog who likes to do things on his own. The cover shows him with his tongue attached to a dragonfly. The story is about his adventures being attached to the dragonfly.

*Tuesday* (Wiesner, 1991). We include this book here although it is mostly wordless. Children enjoy contemplating what is happening as they delve into the illustrations. We talk more about this book when we explore visual literacy later in the chapter.

**Fairy Tales About Frogs.** We start off with the traditional fairy tale *The Frog Prince*. There are numerous versions of this tale. We chose three: a beginning reader text—*The Frog Prince* (Wang, 1986); a more complex version—*The Frog Prince* (Tarcov, 1974); and the most sophisticated version—*The Frog Prince* (Ormerod, 1990). Initially, these books could be used as read-alouds. The Wang version is a good starting point for children to become familiar with the basic story line. It begins with the princess wanting her ball, which has fallen into the water. The frog helps, but only after he secures the promise from the princess that she'll invite him into her house. He eats and sleeps there, although she is not pleased by these events. Then he turns into a prince, as he has been under a spell by a wicked witch, and they live happily ever after.

The Tarcov version is one that most first graders can read on their own after their teacher's introduction. This version has much more dialogue than the other two. And the king reminds the princess repeatedly that she must deliver on her promises. With so much dialogue, this version lends itself to Readers Theater. Readers Theater will allow children repeated practice, which will support fluency development. Plus, they will love performing the parts.

The Ormerod version is the most difficult. It is told in third person, with little dialogue. In this version, it is the queen who reminds her daughter to keep her promises. The frog sleeps in her bed for three nights and when he leaves she finds that she misses him. We recommend using this version as a read-aloud in the first grade. It is also a great source of vocabulary, with words like *miserable*, *shivered*, *troubled*, *enchanted*, and *royal*.

These traditional books are good for exploring story line. For instance, why would a wicked witch turn the prince into a frog? Why a frog? Why not some other animal or insect? Or why would the prince want to marry the princess when she threw him across the room (when he was a frog) and didn't want to keep her promises to him? While there are no right or wrong answers here, the questions stir discussion.

There are also many variations of this fairy tale. We focus on two: *The Frog Prince Continued* (Scieszka, 1991) and *The Frog Princess* (Lewis, 1994). In *The Frog Prince Continued*, the prince and the princess do not live happily ever after. There are several pages describing just how unhappy the Prince was. As children engage with this book they move from one fairy tale to another as the prince meets various witches in his attempt to return to being a frog. At the end of the story the prince and princess both become frogs. We know that children enjoy fractured fairy tales and they lead to direct comparison to the original versions. We also know that in most fractured tales, teachers have to support children with more background information. For instance, in this version, children need to know the fairy tales of Snow White, Sleeping Beauty, Cinderella, and Hansel and Gretel to fully appreciate the Frog Prince; additionally, there is a reference to the King of France that might confuse some children. We also wonder what children may think about the ending of this tale. Do they find it satisfying? Children may compare it to popular culture—a similar plot occurs in the movie *Shrek*.

Scieszka also wrote a short fractured version of *The Frog Prince* in *The Stinky Cheese Man and Other Fairly Stupid Tales* (1992). This tale could be used in comparisons with *The Frog Prince Continued* or *The Frog Princess*.

*The Frog Princess* is not an easy version to follow. It is set in Russia with a tsar instead of a king. There are three princes who are asked to shoot arrows. The finder of each prince's arrow will become that prince's wife. The third prince has his arrow returned by a frog. The prince is inconsolable but marries the frog. Then there are tasks put to the three princesses—a tale within a tale—and the frog princess is the most successful. The frog princess turns into a beautiful woman, Vasilisa the Wise, who leaves her frog skin behind on her pillow when she changes form. The prince burns the frog skin left on the pillow, which, unfortunately, is disastrous for his wife. He must find her a kingdom before they are able to live happily ever after. This book provides an opportunity for charting the many plot lines within a single tale. (See Figure 2.2, for an example.)

### PLOTS WITHIN *THE FROG PRINCESS*

- The princes have to shoot an arrow to find a wife. Two princes find a bride who is a person and the third prince finds a bride who is a frog.

- The tsar wants to know which daughter-in-law is the cleverest. They have to sew and bake.

- When lightning strikes, the frog turns into a princess. The other princesses imitate her at the ball. She can change into a frog or a princess.

- The prince burns the frog skin and the princess turns into ashes. Now the prince has to find a kingdom to save her.

- The prince goes on a quest to find the kingdom. He finds animals along the way and he does not hurt them. Later they help him.

FIGURE 2.2: Plots Within *The Frog Princess*

Both of these books allow for a different exploration on the part of students. *The Frog Princess* challenges children to recognize other stories within its structure. In *The Frog Princess*, children have to reconcile multiple plots in a single tale. On the first reading of these books, we expect that children will primarily focus on the plot. On following readings, children might consider the illustrations, as they are very different in each book. For instance, in *The Frog Princess*, the illustrator provides very detailed illustrations reflecting Russian art. Additionally, it is the only version in which the frog wears clothes. Children might explore why the illustrator chose to dress the frog. Does it have anything to do with the frog's being a girl rather than a boy? In the Ormerod version of the original tale, each page has intricate borders. Children could study the borders and discuss how they add to the story. Do they predict or support the text on the page? Through these discussions students move beyond the literal plot and explore art and how it adds or detracts from the story. Students, in pairs or small groups, could discuss what they note about the illustrations and how they change each interpretation of the story by considering several versions or fractured versions of this fairy tale. Through these explorations, students' attention is brought to the shared effect or synergy of text and illustrations.

## Poems

We have included three volumes of poetry collections for children's exploration. In keeping with the frog theme, we have focused on collections that include a few poems about frogs. You can guide students to understanding poems, pointing out that each word is important and showing students how poets can include facts in their poems as well.

*A Frog Inside My Hat* (Robinson, 1993). This is a wonderful first collection of poems for children, most about animals or children, including one about a frog. Additionally, frogs appear in the illustrations throughout the book. The frog poem in this book does not give information about frogs.

*The Random House Book of Poetry for Children* (Prelutsky, 1983). In this collection we found three poems about frogs. In "The Frog," readers discover that the frog is described in many ways, most not very favorable (e.g., slimy skin). Similar to the frog in the poem in *A Frog Inside My Hat*, this frog is not happy with the names attached to it. After students have read these two poems, they could do an Internet search to explore the reputation of frogs. The other two frog poems in this collection focus on a tree frog and polliwogs. These two poems, we believe, could be used to teach students facts about frogs. By reading these poems, children learn the following:

- There are different kinds of frogs; one kind is a tree frog
- Tree frogs live in elm and oak trees
- Polliwogs live in bogs and turn into frogs

*Greens* (Adoff, 1988). This is a collection of poems about green things. The book is dedicated to Kermit, from *Sesame Street*, for being green. The dedication is a poem about Kermit. We think children will enjoy seeing a book dedicated to a frog.

## Nonfiction

The majority of books we have selected are informational texts. We value the use of informational text with all children, and see it as a direct extension of the core reading selection. We start with the simplest text structure for young children and move to the most complex. A word wall, with picture support, will help highlight important vocabulary as your class moves through these books. You can also hang multiple charts throughout the room with information about frogs in general as well as additional charts with information about different kinds of frogs. Children can also create these charts in personal responses to the books they read or explore. For instance, they might write five fantastic frog facts after exploring several books. If each fact is recorded on a sticky note, children can group and regroup their facts. They might place all facts about the frog's life cycle together, or they might place all facts about different kinds of frogs together.

*Frogs* (MacLulich, 1996). This book, though only 15 pages long and with limited text on each page, is loaded with information. Readers will learn about the many different types of frogs, where they live, what they eat, and how they sound. The book also describes the frog's life cycle. This is a good book to build directly from the core selection. After reading and discussing this book with children, you can co-create charts with students. For example, you might create a chart with information about frogs, one with frog types and one that details the frog life

Frogs
Carolyn MacLulich
for The Australian Museum
SCHOLASTIC

cycle. Where possible we would include photos to support this information. See Figure 2.3 for an example of a chart on types of frogs.

See Figure 2.4 for a chart that targets factual information about frogs. You might also want to include the source of the data so that children can refer back to a particular book for clarification of information.

**TYPES OF FROGS**

| White-lipped frog<br>  Size—long as a fork | White-lipped frogs are as long as a fork<br><br>From *Frogs*, MacLulich, 1996, p.6 |
|---|---|
| Australian tree frog<br>  Size—big as a hand | |
| Buzzing frog<br>  Size—small as a fingernail | |

FIGURE 2.3: Types of Frogs chart

*Frogs and Toads and Tadpoles, Too* (Fowler, 1992). While the text in this book is simple, the ideas are complicated. The book provides descriptions of frogs and also identifies where various frog types live. There are many ideas to discuss. Words

**FACTS ABOUT FROGS**

| What do they look like? | Where do they live? | What do they eat? | Who are their enemies? | What sound do they make? |
|---|---|---|---|---|
| Four fingers on each hand | Damp places (creeks, marshes) | Insects | | Croaking sound with a vocal sac under chin |
| Five toes on each foot | Gardens | Spiders | | |
| Webs of skin between fingers and toes | Trees in the rain forest | Worms | | |

FIGURE 2.4: Facts About Frogs chart

that are highlighted throughout this book are listed on the last page, where each is paired with a photo.

*Life as a Frog* (Parker, 2004). This book provides a wonderful model for children in that it includes a table of contents, a glossary, and an index. As many informational texts are, this book is illustrated with photos. The book is organized into the phases of a frog's life. Each phase is titled with important information listed about it. The book is rich in vocabulary, with new words for children such as *spawn* and *hatch*.

*Frogs* (Driscoll, 1998). This is a simple text that young children can read. They will also be delighted by the illustrations, which share basic information about frogs. This book would serve as an interesting comparison to most of the other factual books about frogs that use photos. We suspect children would not identify it as nonfiction when first viewing it.

*From Tadpole to Frog* (Stewart, 1998). This book is similar to the others in its description of frogs. Unlike the others, it provides much more detail about the life cycle of a frog. Each page shares interesting diagrams and illustrations of the process. Children can use this book to understand how to read diagrams and learn how they connect to the information provided in the text.

*What Am I?* (Butterfield & Ford, 1998). This book is a wonderful riddle about frogs. Each page asks a child to look closely at a part of the frog's body. It also carefully shows how a frog captures an insect with its tongue. The book ends with a series of questions about the content. You might use some of these questions before reading and ask students to carefully listen for the answers. The book also ends with a glossary of important words—many will be familiar to students who have read the other frog books.

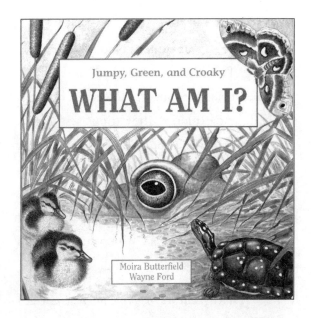

*Fantastic Frogs!* (Robinson, 1999). This is an informational book written as a poem. It may be children's first experience with a poem that is not fictional. Like *Frogs*, this book is illustrated, not photographed. We believe this book would be a great source for writing. Children could choose a frog that Robinson has briefly described and continue with a more elaborate description. At the end of the book, Robinson provides the names for the frogs displayed in the book.

*Red-Eyed Tree Frog* (Cowley, 2006). This book is centered on one frog as it experiences its life in the rain forest. The book is organized around photos and simple text.

*Flashy Fantastic Rain Forest Frogs* (Patent, 1997). This book narrows its focus to frogs that live in the rain forest. In addition to talking about the frogs, it presents important information about rain forests. It includes spectacular vocabulary that children will enjoy learning, such as *predators, canopy, understory,* and *camouflage.* The book relies on illustrations, rather than photos, but they are very complex and children will want to study them for long periods at a time.

*Uncover a Frog* (Bakken, 2006). This book is a three-dimensional look inside a frog. The text is very difficult and will need teacher support. However, children will love exploring the various systems within a frog. There is a wealth of scientific terms, such as *tibiofibula*, *radioulna*, *skull*, *spine*, and *illium*. There are also lots of interesting tidbits of information about frogs, such as "Frogs drink water through their skin, too!"

*Frogs!* (Editors of *Time for Kids*, 2006). This chapter book provides a model for exploring longer books about a single topic. Students learn important information about frogs. They learn about its life cycle. One chapter describes what and how frogs eat. The book also focuses on the possibility of frog extinction and provides a rich vocabulary about frogs. This book is written so that most first graders can read it on their own.

*If You Hopped Like a Frog* (Schwartz, 1999). This book is full of facts about animals and is presented in a clever way that asks children to imagine themselves in the animals' place. Readers learn that if they hopped like a frog, they "could jump from home plate to first base in one mighty leap!" The book ends with the calculations that were used to determine the answers. While young children will not necessarily understand the calculations, they will enjoy learning about connections between animals and themselves.

*Frogs and Toads* (Preston-Mafham, 1999). With photos of more than 100 species of frogs and toads, this book serves as a useful reference text. Most first graders will find the text too difficult to read, but they will enjoy the photos and learning the names of the great variety of species with your support.

*All About Frogs* (Arnosky, 2002). This book shares how frogs grow and live. The author helps children recognize frogs by the sounds they make. The text is easy and the illustrations are similar to paintings, rather than simple drawings.

*How Do Frogs Swallow With Their Eyes?* (Berger & Berger, 2002). This is a question-and-answer book about amphibians. Children will want to know all the answers. And the best part is that the answers are written in a student-friendly way. For example, in response to the title question, the authors write:

> *Easily. When swallowing a big mouthful of food, a frog blinks with its eyes. The blinking pushes the frog's huge eyeballs down on the top of its mouth. This helps squeeze the food in its mouth into its throat. WHOOSH! Down goes its meal!* (p. 4)

The book moves beyond its exploration of frogs to include all amphibians. Students will have the background knowledge of frogs to help them as they explore this larger, more complex topic area.

These books and others like them that you may select offer students multiple opportunities to explore narrative, poetry, and informational text about frogs. As students explore these books for information, they also learn about different genres. And within the genre of informational text, they come to understand that some books are organized by description while others are organized by a time sequence or a question-and-answer format.

## Writing Connections

We mentioned a few suggestions for writing as we shared frog books. We believe there are multiple opportunities for students to write as scientists throughout this exploration. Following are some ideas for incorporating writing into the lessons.

- Teacher and students create charts that share information about frogs.
- Teacher and students create content vocabulary word wall.
- Students create journals about frog information and vocabulary that they collect as they read.

- Students use learning logs to record their observations of tadpoles turning into frogs.
- Students do a quick sketch and then write about what they observe. They also note the date so that they can write a sequential description of this process.
- Students create a frog report. This report could be constructed with a fact on each page.

The report mentioned in the last point could be labeled "Five Fantastic Frog Facts." Each page would include an illustration and a fact about a frog. An engaging way for students to create it might be with paper folded so that each page is a bit longer than the previous one, like a flip chart. (See Figure 2.5.) By using this organizational format, children can view all of their facts at one time. You may also want students to replicate some of the frog books they have explored by including a table of contents and a glossary. Students might also create frog reports that explain the frog life cycle or different kinds of frogs. This study provides a perfect opportunity for students to generate a report or one of their first informational text pieces.

In addition to informational writing, students can also participate in narrative or poetry writing explorations. For instance, children can create their own Froggy or Frog and Toad stories. And to support comparative skills, students might create a diamante poem about frogs and toads or about two different kinds of frogs. In Figure 2.6, we share a simple variation of the diamante

## FORMAT FOR REPORT

**Poison Dart Frog**

| | |
|---|---|
| Fact 1 | Its poison could kill a person. |
| Fact 2 | It is bright green, pink, or gold. |
| Fact 3 | It begins as a tiny egg. |
| Fact 4 | It is cold blooded. |
| Fact 5 | It is an amphibian. |

Paper is cut, folded, and stapled at the top. Title is the shortest sheet. Each following fact sheet is longer than the one preceding it.

FIGURE 2.5: Format for Report

**DIAMANTE POEMS FOR FROG AND TOAD**

| "Frog and Toad" | "Frog and Toad" |
|---|---|
| Frog | Frog |
| Clean, helpful | Shiny, smooth |
| Storyteller, friend, lazy, sad | Marshes, wet place, dry land, desert |
| Messy, procrastinates | Rough, bumpy |
| Toad | Toad |

FIGURE 2.6: Diamante Poems for Frog and Toad

structure. (We include two poems—one for the characters Frog and Toad and one for an informational comparison.) Children begin with the topic name. They follow with two adjectives to describe their topic word. The middle line begins with two descriptive words or phrases for the first word and then ends with two descriptive words or phrases for the last word. That line is followed by two adjectives to describe the final word. The final word is the topic being compared to the first word. This poem format lends itself to comparisons.

## Author or Illustrator Studies

For an exploration of the author Fay Robinson (*Fantastic Frogs*, *A Frog Inside My Hat*), we return to the core program anthology. The anthology features a brief overview of Robinson, as well as a selection of her writing. Children learn that she loves to write about snakes, frogs, and other creepy things. Robinson began her career as a teacher before becoming a writer. She used to bring tadpoles into her classroom.

She has written numerous books on science. See Figure 2.7 for a list of many of her books that students could explore. Students may notice a similarity in many of her titles; she often uses an adjective to describe the topic. Robinson's books also feature illustrations rather than photographs. Many of her books belong to the Rookie Readers series by Scholastic, so the reading is not challenging for first graders.

As students explore her books, they will learn that Robinson is most interested in science, especially insects, spiders, snakes, birds, and amphibians. Her topics support teachers in simple science investigations. They also provide students with a model of informational writing.

Recently she began writing books about crafts. You may use these books to show her versatility in writing, but the focus should be on her science books.

Robinson uses many interesting adjectives and often provides comparisons such as *droopy folds* (*Fantastic Frogs!*, 1999, p. 24) or *eyes like fire* (p. 25). As children continue to explore her books, we are sure that a classroom list of her titles and of the details within them will grow and children will come to know more about this talented author.

## Extension of the Core Reading Program Theme

The theme for this unit is Take a Closer Look. As children explore the numerous books about frogs and the additional books by Robinson, they'll be delighted by the illustrations and photos. To enhance students' visual experience, you might use photos and illustrations for student study. Each of the books shared is a great source for visual renderings. You might share these illustrative materials through PowerPoint with enlargements so that students can see the details more clearly. On page 42, we offer Web sites where students can explore the visual aspects of frogs in detail as well.

An illustration that is folded into quarters would provide a study in close-ups. Children could examine one quarter at a time and describe what they see before considering the whole.

It's also a good idea to bring in tadpoles or other creatures for students to study on a daily basis. As students observe these creatures and record information in their learning logs, they will note details from their careful examination. This type of study will allow them to more fully understand the life cycle of a frog and to observe and record as a scientist would.

**FAY ROBINSON BOOKS**

*We Love Fruit!*

*Vegetables, Vegetables!*

*Recycle That!*

*Too Much Trash!*

*Where Do Puddles Go?*

*Meet My Mouse*

*Great Snakes!*

*Mighty Spiders!*

*Amazing Lizards!*

*A Dinosaur Named Sue: The Find of the Century*

*Fabulous Frogs!*

*Creepy Beetles*

*Singing Robins*

*Flying Bats*

*Wacky Fish*

*Faucet Fish*

*Chinese New Year—A Time for Parades, Family, and Friends*

*Halloween—Costumes and Treats on All Hallows' Eve*

*Christmas Crafts*

*Halloween Crafts*

*Halloween—Disfraces y Golosinas en la Víspera de Todos los Santos*

*Father's Day Crafts*

*Hispanic-American Crafts Kids Can Do!*

FIGURE 2.7: Fay Robinson Books

## Vocabulary Extensions

We believe it is important for students to constantly add to a content word wall as they explore frogs. Each book repeats and extends this scientific vocabulary, so students have many opportunities for practice.

We suggest that because of the scientific nature of so many of the books, you ask students to carefully scrutinize illustrations or photos and then generate five words a scientist might use to describe them. Students could share their words with a partner so that the whole class is engaged. For instance, a child might say "a climber, hooded eyes, bumpy skin," and so on. These words could be shared with the class or put on a chart so that students begin to fully understand how a scientist might think and describe what she's seeing.

## Ties to Content Areas Such as Social Studies and Science

The study of frogs provides a foundation for a more extensive study of animal life cycles. First graders might move to an exploration of butterflies and then make connections between the frog's and the butterfly's life cycles. Check on your content standards to determine further connections to your science curriculum.

## Visual Literacy Extensions

This frog exploration is filled with opportunities for visual literacy extensions. Following are a few possibilities.

- Revisit the book *Tuesday* (Wiesner, 1991). To begin to understand this text, children need a lengthy time exploring each page. There is so much to take in—frogs that fly and do stunts, those who sit quietly and watch television. Children might discuss the frogs' evening adventures and then discuss why they return to a pond. To begin these discussions, you might enlarge one page and have children chat about what they notice. Then divide the class into small groups and have each group focus on a different page of the text. Then ask each group to offer ideas about what they think this story is about and how they made their decisions through careful observation.

- Compare a book that is illustrated with drawings to one with photographs. Children can record what they notice in photos that they don't see in illustrations and vice versa. They can also evaluate why an author would choose one over the other.

- Children could create trading cards. Have them place a frog on the front of each card. Then they can list on the back three interesting facts about the frog. Laminate the cards for children or purchase plastic trading-card sleeves and cut them apart so a child can place his or her card in a sleeve for protection. The goal of the activity is for the child to carefully represent the chosen frog as accurately as possible, making sure all of the important details are included. See Figure 2.8 for an example.

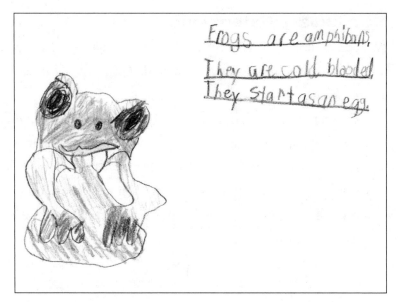

FIGURE 2.8: Frog trading card

## Connections to Technology

You can further expand the study on frogs by making connections to technology. Following is a list of Web sites with brief descriptions.

- **Read Write Think (www.readwritethink.org)** This Web site offers activities for teachers that are supported with research. Each lesson is clearly detailed, with all supportive materials available. The site also identifies national standards that are met. We checked out the lesson The Frog Beyond the Fairy Tale Character, which is an interesting worksheet from The Somewhat Amusing World of Frogs Web site (www.csu.edu.au/faculty/commerce/account/frogs/frog.htm). This sheet asks students to respond with true or false to statements like "Frogs tend to jump and toads tend to walk." These questions provide a focus for students as they investigate multiple books about frogs. The other strength of this Web site is its full Web resource gallery.

- **Scott Foresman Reading Headquarters (www.sfreading.com)** This site features the Scott Foresman core reading program. Click on the anthology selection. We chose the Tadpole to Frog text. This led to a page titled Frogtastic Facts. Children can choose to explore the frog life cycle, facts about frogs and amphibians, frogs around the world, stories, poems, and jokes, and other interesting information. It also lists multiple sites that children might visit to find more frog information.

- **All About Frogs (www.allaboutfrogs.org/)** This site has a variety of information about frogs, including weird frog facts, frogs in the news, international frogs, and a frog art gallery.

There is also a section describing frog myths. This site is best for teachers to visit to find information to share with children, rather than a site that children visit.

- **Exploratorium: Frogs (www.exploratorium.edu/frogs)** This site has articles about frogs and extensive links to other frog sites. Click on Frog Tracker to listen to the sounds of frogs. Children move a flashlight around and when they land on a frog, the frog makes a sound and the name of the frog appears.

- **Enchanted Learning (www.enchantedlearning.com/subjects/amphibians/frogprintout.shtml)** This site allows you to print out the frog life cycle for student study.

- **Nature Sounds (www.naturesound.com/frogs/frogs.html)** There are numerous photos of frogs at this Web site. Children can view a frog and listen to its sound.

- **Kiddy House (www.kiddyhouse.com/Themes/frogs)** This site provides a vast amount of information about frogs. Teachers can go here for songs and poems as well.

- **National Geographic (www.nationalgeographic.com)** This site has a wealth of information about animals, places, and so on. After arriving at the site, we typed in "frogs" and numerous links came up. One link took us directly to an issue of the *National Geographic Explorer* student magazine featuring an interesting article about freaky frogs. There are many downloads available as well.

# Connections to First-Grade Literacy Standards

In this section we list several of the national and state standards that are targeted through the core reading and extended reading and writing programs described in this chapter. We have shortened the full descriptions of the standards. The full descriptions of national standards are available on the International Reading Association (www.reading.org) and/or National Council of Teachers of English (www.ncte.org) Web sites. State standards are available on state department of education Web sites.

## International Reading Association and National Council of Teachers of English Literacy Standards

**Standard 1.** Students read a wide range of print and nonprint texts to build understanding of texts. These texts are fiction and nonfiction.

**Standard 3.** Students apply a wide range of strategies to comprehend, interpret, evaluate, and appreciate texts.

**Standard 4.** Students adjust their use of spoken, written, and visual language to communicate effectively.

**Standard 5.** Students use a wide variety of strategies as they write and use different writing process elements.

**Standard 6.** Students apply knowledge of language structure, language conventions, media techniques, figurative language, and genre to create, critique, and discuss print and nonprint texts.

**Standard 7.** Students conduct research on issues and interests.

**Standard 8.** Students use a variety of technological and information resources.

**Standard 11.** Students participate as knowledgeable, reflective, creative, and critical members of literacy communities.

**Standard 12.** Students use spoken, written, and visual language to accomplish their own purposes.

## California Language Arts Standards for First Grade

We have chosen selected language arts standards for first graders in California that are clearly met in the core reading program selection and the extended activities. In each chapter, we identify a different state's language arts standards so that we can document how the suggested activities meet state expectations. Through this exploration, you can feel assured that you are targeting the learning and teaching expectations of your state.

Children are expected to accomplish the following:

- Identify the title and author of a reading selection
- Create and state rhyming words
- Read and generate word families; distinguish short and long vowel sounds in single-syllable words
- Classify categories of words
- Identify texts that use a sequence
- Respond to who, what, when, where, and how questions
- Relate prior knowledge to textual information
- Retell central ideas of simple expository or narrative passages
- Identify the elements of plot, setting, and characters in a story

- Describe the role of authors and illustrators
- Recollect, talk, and write about books
- Select a focus when writing
- Write brief expository descriptions (www.cde.ca.gov/be/st/ss/scgrade1.asp)

## California Science Standards

- Students know that animals live in different habitats and need water and food
- Students can ask meaningful questions and conduct experiments; they can draw pictures to portray what they are studying and record observations (www.cde.ca.gov/be/st/ss/scgrade1.asp)

Importantly, teachers can address their state standards as well as national standards when they extend their core reading program. We recommend that before choosing or developing extensions, you investigate your standards so that they target the most appropriate activities to support student learning.

# CHAPTER 3

# *S*econd-Grade Possibilities

*A teacher's view of literature and learning is the greatest determinant of what will happen in a classroom where children read real books. A specific view guides their judgment of what is significant and of value, in both how texts to be read are selected and how the reading of those texts is approached.*

—Ralph Peterson and Maryann Eeds, *Grand Conversations*

As we did in our first-grade exploration, here we also selected a text from a second-grade core reading program, in this case Harcourt Trophies (2003). In this chapter, we describe core reading possibilities and expectations with this text selection, and then move to literature-based curriculum that extends and deepens children's understanding of this text and related texts. For this exploration we are going to put the theme, Imagine That, offered in the core anthology, in the foreground as a way to organize instruction and material selection. We include other possibilities as well so you can view multiple ways of extending a simple core text selection.

## The Core Reading Program

Theme 1 in second-grade Harcourt Trophies is Imagine That. We chose this theme because it is filled with wonderful possible extensions for second graders. Within this theme in the core anthology are five major text selections. These include *The Day Jimmy's Boa Ate the Wash* (Noble, 1992); *How I Spent My Summer Vacation* (Teague, 1997); *Dear Mr. Blueberry* (James, 1996); *Cool Ali* (Poydar, 1996); and *The Emperor's Egg* (Jenkins, 2003). The books represent various genres, including fantasy, informational text, and realistic fiction, and all are published as books outside of the core anthology. These books serve as a strong base for core reading instruction and for literature-based extensions. While we chose *The Day Jimmy's Boa Ate the Wash*, any of the others could have been selected as the benchmark text and you would easily be able to extend the curriculum in constructive ways with them. *The Day Jimmy's Boa Ate the Wash* is written by Trinka Noble and is illustrated by Steven Kellogg, who has written many other books for children to explore. His books extend children's thinking into math and other genres like tall tales, and his work supports students in understanding the subtleties apparent in fiction and how they might employ them in writing fanciful texts. (See Children's Literature Cited, pages 119–120.)

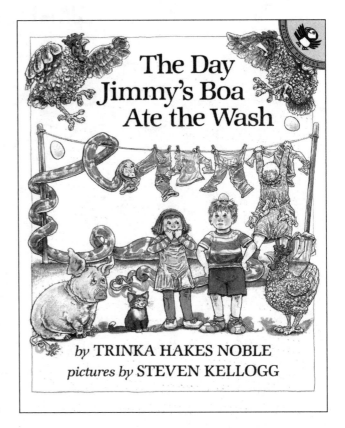

*The Day Jimmy's Boa Ate the Wash* has numerous teaching and learning expectations associated with it as described in the teacher's edition. Following is a listing of the curricular expectations surrounding this fantasy text selection.

## Comprehension

- Access prior knowledge related to understanding cause-and-effect relationships; students should think about cause and effect and when a story directly provides evidence of this relationship and when it has to be implied by the reader
- Create a cause-and-effect chart with teacher help as they read text; see Figure 3.1 for an example
- Practice making and confirming predictions as they read through this selection

| CAUSE | EFFECT |
|---|---|
| Jimmy brought his boa to the farm. | The boa frightened a hen that laid an egg on Jenny's head. |
| Jenny thought Tommy threw the egg. | Jenny threw an egg at Tommy. |
| The egg hit Marianne. | Marianne threw an egg at Jenny and missed and hit Jimmy. |

FIGURE 3.1: Cause-and-effect table

- Engage in prereading strategies and predict what might happen on a field trip to the farm; then read designated pages and adjust predictions to the field trip described in this story
- Understand that this story is a fantasy—reread the story and identify events that could or could not happen in real life; at the beginning of the text, observe things that animals do not typically do and things on the farm that are different from typical farms
- Establish a purpose for reading; in this case, the purpose is for enjoyment

## Word Knowledge
### Vocabulary
- Become familiar with these words: *boring*, *ducked*, *sense*, *suppose*, and *tractor*
### Phonics
- Practice the vowel diphthongs of *ou* and *ow* in words like *mouth* and *how*
### Word Structure
- Practice the suffixes *-ful* and *-less* in words like *disgraceful* and *soundless*
### High-Frequency Words
- Read with fluency the words *cow*, *hen*, *mean*, *started*, and *wife*

## Fluency
- Reread the text and/or listen to it on CD and follow along with the text; students who are below grade level in reading echo-read following the teacher's modeling

## Writing
- Consider the way Noble started this story—"How was your class trip to the farm?" "Oh . . . Boring . . . kind of dull . . . until the cow started crying"—as a way to write stronger beginnings
- Visit the author and illustrator sites at Harcourt to learn more about authors and illustrators and how they go about writing and illustrating (www.harcourtschool.com)
- Make a poster about all the things children did to cause trouble in the story; create field trip rules for a safer trip
- Pretend to be TV reporters and interview the children on the field trip; write up their findings as an interview.
- Practice using pronouns in their writing.

There are many teaching points centered on this single selection. Although there are multiple opportunities for direct instruction throughout the selection, the authors of this series provide students additional practice both with teacher scaffolding in small-group settings and independently through practice activities. Specific skills and strategies are reinforced or enriched in small-group instruction with leveled text that extends the theme of the core text selection. For independent practice, while small groups of students are meeting with the teacher, students can listen to the text read on CD by an expert reader and/or do fluency activities, practice pages in workbooks, and Web-based activities at the center.

*The Day Jimmy's Boa Ate the Wash* is the major selection for a week's worth of instruction. Even with an entire week, you'll need to decide the most important strategy or skill to teach directly, the best skill or strategy to be practiced with a teacher or peer, and the best activities for independent practice. These decisions might vary with the skill level of individual students. For instance, students who are slow readers might spend more time with fluency practice, students who struggle with inferential comprehension might engage in more directed instruction with their teacher, and so on.

# The Extended Literacy Curriculum

*The Day Jimmy's Boa Ate the Wash* offers an amazing number of ways to enrich the literacy curriculum. Certainly, author or illustrator studies are important and can easily be supported through the numerous texts written by Noble and those illustrated by Kellogg. This book serves as a foundation for a larger exploration into the theme, Imagine That. For this theme we selected many books in which a basic story is expanded through a child's imagination. We see this as an opportunity for children to understand how simple plots—like a field trip—can be expanded into make-believe tales through writing and illustrations. We also identified many tall tales for children to explore since Kellogg has retold so many of them and they support the theme of imagination.

## Reading Connections

### Fiction

A wealth of books support connections to the benchmark selection. Here we include stories to support a genre study of tall tales; later in the chapter, we have a more substantial review of literature with an imagination theme under Extension of the Core Reading Program Theme.

Tall tales are usually based on a real person but are greatly exaggerated. These stories are usually humorous, but they often hold some truth, such as the importance of being quick-witted or brave in difficult circumstances.

In *Children's Literature*, Mitchell (2003) identifies the following seven key criteria to determine whether a book is a tall tale:

- Physical attributes of the main character are exaggerated
- Accomplishments of the main character are exaggerated
- Winning and competition are emphasized
- Colorful language is used
- Humor is woven throughout
- The main character is helpful
- The story is creative

These criteria help illuminate this particular part of the traditional literature genre. Children, with the support of their teacher, may want to create tall-tale charts in which they describe each of the criteria for particular tall tales. Later, they might choose to compare two tall tales or two characters from two tall tales (see Figure 3.2).

When we searched for tall tales, we found that many interesting ones are written and illustrated by Steven Kellogg. As students learn about tall tales, they also have multiple exposures to the work of Kellogg.

| PECOS BILL | JOHNNY APPLESEED |
|---|---|
| As a baby he moved from New England to east Texas. | He was born in the fall of 1774 in Massachusetts; later he moved west. |
| He was adopted by a coyote family and he became like them. | His house was crowded and noisy so he escaped to the woods. |
| He was the world's greatest cowboy. | He was the world's best appleseed planter. |
| He invented cows with short legs on one side so they could stand securely on a slope. | He was the best at cutting down trees. |
| He was ambushed by a rattlesnake, but Pecos Bill squeezed the snake until the poison left his body. | His feet were as tough as an elephant's hide so he was not hurt when a rattlesnake bit him. |

FIGURE 3.2: Comparison of characters

*Cloudy With a Chance of Meatballs* (Barrett, 1978). This story is an old favorite. The book begins with the children eating a breakfast that Grandpa prepared. Later that night Grandpa shares a tall tale with the children about the tiny town of Chewandswallow. This is a perfect book to explore tall tales. While most tall tales are based on a real person, this one is based on a fictional unusual town. Children might decide that based on the criteria for a tall tale, Grandpa really didn't tell one.

*John Henry* (Lester, 1994). John Henry is another tall-tale hero, an African American who is born into the world big and strong. He grows to be the greatest "steel-driver" in the mid-century push to extend the railroads across the mountains to the West. When the owner of the railroad buys a steam-powered hammer to do the work of his crew, John Henry challenges the inventor to a contest: John Henry versus the steam hammer.

*Johnny Appleseed* (Kellogg, 1988). This well-known tall tale encapsulates the life of Johnny Appleseed, who planted apple trees across the U.S. and did more than any other person to popularize the virtues of the apple.

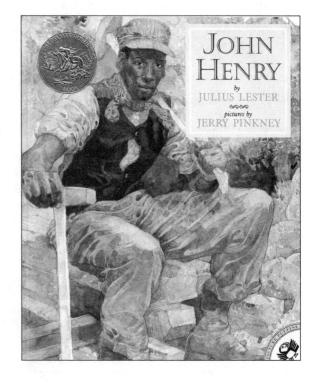

*Pecos Bill* (Kellogg, 1986). Pecos Bill is a mythical cowboy who can stave off rattlesnakes and ride tornados as he conquers the wild, wild West.

*Library Lil* (Williams, 1997). This is an unusual tall tale of a librarian who was very strong and made a community into readers. Unlike other tall tales, this one is not about past events; rather it takes place in a current setting. Children will need to decide whether it fits the criteria of a tall tale.

*Sally Ann Thunder Ann Whirlwind Crockett: A Tall Tale* (Kellogg, 1999). Sally Ann, even as a toddler, is kind and strong and has superhuman strength; she can outrun rabbits and out-swim otters. And once she marries Davy Crockett, she even dispenses with all alligators from Minnesota to New Orleans, sweeping them up in a tornado.

*Mike Fink* (Kellogg, 1998). Another merry tall tale that features Fink, grizzly-bear wrestler and King of the Mississippi River Keelboatmen.

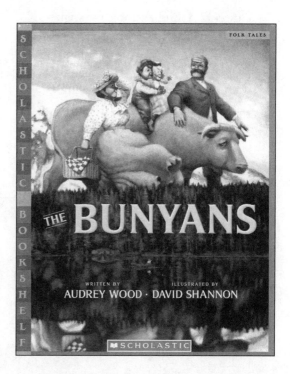

*Paul Bunyan* (Kellogg, 1985). Probably the best-known superhero of all the tall tales, Paul Bunyan tamed the West with Babe, his blue ox, by his side.

*The Bunyans* (Wood, 1996). This book shares the whole story of Paul Bunyan and his family. It explains how Paul Bunyan was responsible for many of the wonders in the U.S. It could serve as a comparison text to Kellogg's *Paul Bunyan.*

## Nonfiction

We have targeted two nonfiction areas for children to explore. The first centers on snakes and is a smaller extension to the core selection for students to investigate. Second-grade students will be excited just to look through these books, as the illustrations are quite remarkable. On second and third perusals, students will learn interesting facts about snakes that they will want to share with classmates. You could more formally organize this investigation by asking students to create reports or posters of interesting facts about snakes to share with other students.

*Great Snakes* (Robinson, 1996). This is a counting book as well as a book that provides basic information about snakes. This book is classified as a Hello Reader, so second graders should have no difficulty with the text.

*Slinky Scaly Slithery Snakes* (Patent, 2003). This text shares the many patterns and sizes of snakes. The illustrations are scientifically accurate and depict snakes as they hunt, hide, and reproduce.

*Find the Snake* (Foley, 2000). This offering is organized with a table of contents. Children look for snakes in various places, including in the sand and trees. The text is simple, so children have no difficulty focusing on the content.

*Snakes: Long, Longer, Longest* (Pallotta, 2006). This book details information about snakes. The illustrations are engaging and support children's learning of information about snakes.

*The Snake Book* (DK Publishing, 1997). This book provides numerous photos of snakes and fascinating details about them. The reading level is more difficult than in the other books, but children interested in snakes will find it hard to put down.

*Snakes* (Simon, 1994). This book also provides many details about snakes, but relies on drawings rather than illustrations.

*All About Rattlesnakes* (Arnosky, 2002). This book is one in Arnosky's All About series. It provides information about rattlesnakes, and is illustrated with watercolors filled with detail.

The second nonfiction exploration is a math investigation. Kellogg has illustrated three books dealing with number concepts. They are *How Much Is a Million?* (Schwartz, (1985), *If You Made a Million* (Schwartz, 1989), and *Millions to Measure* (Schwartz, 2003). In *How Much Is a Million?* children learn about the concept of a million. Schwartz shares ways to compare a million to other numerical concepts, such as that it would take 23 days to count to a million or that it would take 70 pages filled with tiny stars to represent a million. He moves from the concept of a million to a billion later in the book. The book *If You Made a Million* teaches children about money, including the concept of interest. The book also carries the message that making money involves making choices. Schwartz includes notes at the end of the book to help teachers and students with the concepts of interest, checking, and loans.

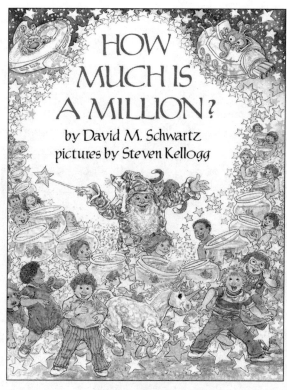

*Millions to Measure* traces the development of standard units of measure for distance, weight, and volume, then describes the development of the metric system in the late 1700s. An appendix offers more in-depth information about the metric system.

We envision these three books as extensions of the math curriculum. We know that students will read and reread these books as they explore the content and illustrations. You might even make use of Marvelosissimo, the mathematical magician who shares information in these books, within your own classroom to explain new mathematic concepts to students.

## Writing Connections

For extending writing beyond the core program expectations, we targeted two activities. The first involves considering how authors start their stories. For this extension, students create charts that record the beginning sentences from each tall tale or from any of Kellogg's books. (See Figure 3.3 for an example.) Then students could consider a piece of their own writing in progress. Each student would then think about his or her first sentence and rewrite it to be more inviting, similar to the initial sentences that are recorded on their chart.

| STORY | FIRST SENTENCE |
|---|---|
| *Where the Wild Things Are* | The night Max wore his wolf suit and made mischief of one kind and another his mother called him "Wild Thing!" and Max said, "I'll eat you up!" |
| *Will's Mammoth* | Will loved mammoths . . . . Woolly mammoths. |
| *Monster Mama* | Patrick Edward was a wonderful boy, but his mother was a monster. |
| *Pecos Bill* | Back in the rugged pioneer days when Pecos Bill was a baby . . . . |
| *Is Your Mama a Llama?* | "Is your mama a llama?" |
| *Chicken Little* | "Poultry coming," announced Foxy Loxy, as he spotted Chicken Little skipping down the road. |

FIGURE 3.3: Story beginnings

A second writing activity centers on having students write their own fanciful tale. We suggest students take a routine event, such as coming to school, doing homework, or playing with a friend, as the organizing event of their story. First, each student drafts a simple plotline—what happened first, second, and so on. Then they deliberate on their characters. They create descriptions of them that include physical attributes as well as personality characteristics. Students might even be encouraged to complete quick sketches of their characters. Once these aspects are completed, the fun begins. They revise their simple plot by adding make-believe events. Their characters might even develop pretend characteristics.

We share two examples of this kind of imaginary writing. The first comes from Mary Paradise, who wrote and illustrated *Imaginary Insects* (1998). Her book is about insects that are happy because "There is no insect spray here!" (p. 1). Each page of her book shows insects playing and flying. She even includes insects from outer space.

The second sample comes from second grader Kennady, who wrote about her dog's ability to communicate with her. Her teacher asked her to tell her fantasy story with the use of dialogue. Figure 3.4 shares a section where Kennady focused on the event of bringing a new dog into her family.

## Lula Can Talk

I just got a new puppy, her name is Lula. We named her Lula because of her silly personality. She is very jumpy and cute. We knew she was special when we first saw her but we couldn't figure out why. One day I finally found out. It was strange but Lula once spoke English!

"Hi!" said a squeaky voice behind me. I turned around and saw my puppy Lula. "Lula" I asked, "What's my name?" "Don't wear it out!" cried Lula. "Did you just talk to me?" "Sure did," said Lula. I thought I was dreaming. I asked, "So how do you like your new home?" Lula jumped on my lap and said, "It's heaven but when I have an accident you come running and start yelling at me." I blushed. "Yeah we really need that new dog door." Lula barked. "Can I ask you another question?" "Sure." "What was your birth name?" "Rain Salad." "Rain Salad?" I questioned. "Yep" yelped Lula. "My mom's name was Autumn Rain and my dad's name was Tater Salad. If you put them together you get Rain Salad." "One more question Lula. Do you like your new family?" Lula smiled. I took that as a yes before Lula jumped on my lap. She said, "One tip for you, Kennady. When I put my ears back that means I'm happy to see you."

I haven't heard Lula talk since then. I think Lula was excited to be with someone new. In her excitement she told me everything I needed to know about her. Sometimes when she barks I can hear a little voice saying, "I love you Kennady." Maybe I am dreaming. What I do know is whenever I see her ears go back I know she is happy to see me.

FIGURE 3.4: Second grader Kennady's fantasy story

## Author or Illustrator Studies

*The Day Jimmy's Boa Ate the Wash* (Noble, 1992) is a strong starting place for exploring the work of the book's illustrator, Steven Kellogg. Students might begin with Kellogg as an illustrator before studying him as an author-illustrator, and in particular investigate how he takes simple stories and embellishes them with his imagination. The following books provide a strong foundation for this exploration. Many center on Jimmy's boa and its adventures. Children might explore constants in Kellogg's work, such as his drawings of animals and the movement he achieves in his drawings.

Trinka Noble's "Jimmy's Boa" Books Illustrated by Steven Kellogg:

    *The Day Jimmy's Boa Ate the Wash*

    *Jimmy's Boa and the Big Splash Birthday Bash*

    *Jimmy's Boa Bounces Back*

    *Jimmy's Boa and the Bungee Jump Slam Dunk*

Other Books Illustrated by Kellogg:

    Bayer, J. *A, My Name Is Alice*

    Brooks A. *Frogs Jump! A Counting Book*

    Erlich, A. *Leo, Zack, and Emmie Together Again*

    Guarino, D. *Is Your Mama a Llama?*

    Kinerk, R. *Clorinda Takes Flight*

    Mahy, M. *The Boy Who Was Followed Home*

    Mahy, M. *Rattlebang Picnic*

    Martin, B. *A Beastly Story*

    Massie, D. *The Baby Beebee Bird*

    Paxton, T. *Engelbert the Elephant*

    Robb, L. *Snuffles and Snouts*

    Ryder, J. *Big Bear Ball*

    Thurber, J. *The Great Quillow*

From this foundation (which does not by any means include all of the books illustrated by Kellogg), children can go on to explore books written and illustrated by Kellogg. We have listed first Kellogg's books about Pinkerton, a character that developed from Kellogg's own dog. Students can visit Kellogg's Web site (www.stevenkellogg.com) to see him with the real Pinkerton.

    *A Rose for Pinkerton*

    *Tallyho, Pinkerton*

    *Pinkerton, Behave*

    *A Penguin Pup for Pinkerton*

    *Prehistoric, Pinkerton*

    *Pinkerton and Friends*

Children can also explore many of Kellogg's other books.

    *Chicken Little*

    *The Christmas Witch*

*Give the Dog a Bone*

*I Was Born About 10,000 Years Ago*

*Jack and the Beanstalk*

*The Missing Mitten Mystery*

*The Mysterious Tadpole*

*Can I Keep Him?*

*The Island of the Skog*

*Best Friends*

*The Three Little Pigs*

*The Three Sillies*

*Yankee Doodle*

*A-Hunting We Will Go!*

There are several ways that children might explore Kellogg as an illustrator. First, they could create a chart and record the animals that Kellogg chooses to illustrate as a way to determine the importance of animals to him. Most of his animals appear in clothing, and students might pursue why this is so. Or they could explore how many of his books feature a snake. Second, children could look at how he adds illustration boxes in many of his texts, a technique he uses in *The Missing Mitten Mystery* and *Chicken Little*. Third, each student in a class might choose one book illustrated by Kellogg. Within this book they would narrow their focus to just one page and record all of the details drawn by Kellogg. One way to help with targeting the detail is to give students a piece of paper folded into fourths with one quarter-section cut out. Students place this paper over the page so they can carefully study only one quarter of the illustration at a time. Finally, students might peruse the whole book and discover how Kellogg adds movement to his illustrations; for example, in *The Missing Mitten Mystery*, Kellogg draws puppy paw prints in the snow to show the puppy running.

Once students have studied Kellogg as an illustrator, they may want to list the characters he showcases in his books, which are often animals. They may want to study the way he begins his stories to reinforce the idea about great beginning sentences. They may want to visit his Web site (www.stevenkellogg.com) and read about what he has to say about his writing. He discusses the importance of adding humor to his books and how he values the picture book, in which illustrations and text enhance one another. Each of these investigations will provide students with a more thorough understanding of an author and illustrator and will then support students in the thinking that is centered on their own writing and reading.

# Extension of the Core Reading Program Theme

For this extension we have selected books where the plot shares a child's experience but then imagination makes it much more than a simple event. We begin with a classic: *Where the Wild Things Are*.

*Where the Wild Things Are* (Sendak, 1991). Many second-grade students will already be familiar with this book, although we doubt they will have explored it in the depth we suggest. First, engage children in just hearing this wonderful story again. Then ask children to think about the simple plot that organizes this story— a child, Max, is placed in his bedroom as punishment and goes somewhere else in his imagination. Then reread the text and invite children to focus

on how Sendak enlarges this story through imagination. Children might talk about the characters or how Sendak pushes Max over a sea to get to the wild things. You could page through the book slowly and just consider the illustrations. Children might need scaffolding to notice how Sendak enlarges each illustration as the story becomes more whimsical. For instance, when the wild rumpus begins, the illustrations cover the entire page with no room for words. Later, when Max's room returns to normal, the story returns to just one page of illustration. Children may want to return to this close viewing of the book during independent time so that they can more carefully study the craft of Sendak.

*Will's Mammoth* (Martin, 1989). This book is similar in structure to *Where the Wild Things Are*. It begins with Will drawing in his very messy bedroom. On the walls are many drawings of mammoths and throughout the room there are mammoths everywhere, even on a pair of underpants left on the floor. Most of the book is wordless but it begins with Will's parents telling him that mammoths disappeared ten thousand years ago. Even though Will hears his parents, he does not believe them. The remainder of the book is filled with beautiful images of Will playing with mammoths. The book ends with Will's imaginary return for dinner. After viewing this book, children might discuss how the author and illustrator collaborated to form this story, which is mainly told through illustration. Children might also compare this story to *Where the Wild Things Are*. Also, as a direct extension of the goals of the core anthology, students could create a chart in which they record the first sentences of books that share in this theme. Through this charting, they can compare how published authors bring readers into their imaginary stories. See Figure 3.3 (page 56) for a sample.

*Monster Mama* (Rosenberg, 1993). Patrick has a very interesting mother. While the illustrations show that they live in a house, the text presents his mother living in a cave. Patrick is sent to get dessert for dinner and on the way three boys decide to take and eat the dessert he bought. They wind up back at his house where his mother, with the help of the boys, produces a very large dessert. In this book as well as the others, the illustrations are amazing. Children will want to spend time just looking at all of the details. This text is sure to spark much discussion about the truth of Patrick's mother.

*There's a Nightmare in My Closet* (Mayer, 1968). This is another book that takes place in a young boy's bedroom. As the boy goes to bed, he closes his closet door so the nightmare cannot get out. However, it does get out and eventually finds its way to the boy's bed, where the boy tucks it in. As this monster settles in the bed, other monsters begin to come out of the closet. The illustrations in this book are simpler than those in the previous texts shared. The focus shifts to the facial illustrations of the monster and the boy. At this point, we think it would be interesting to revisit the previous stories listed in this theme. You might ask children what they think about this selection of main characters, and why in each story a boy character is featured.

We also provide one simple writing extension for this book. Each child gets one sheet of paper that is folded in half, lengthwise, to create a door shape. On the outside, children draw a closet door. On the inside they draw a monster and describe it in detail. See Figure 3.5 for an example.

*Gila Monsters Meet You at the Airport* (Sharmat, 1987). This is a book with a more subtle use of imagination. One boy is moving from the eastern U.S. to the West. Throughout the book he shares his perceptions of what the West might be like. Children could list the misconceptions he acknowledges and then provide more accurate information about the West and the East.

*Night Noises* (Fox, 1989). This is a book about Lily Laceby, a woman who lives with her old dog. She falls

FIGURE 3.5: Monster in a Closet Reading-Writing Extension

asleep in her chair near the fire. The dog hears noises, but Lily Laceby sleeps through it all. Finally, at the end of the story, her dog barks, which wakes her up. She opens the door and finds her family there to honor her with a surprise party. While this story is simple in plot, it offers children a sense of enjoyment through its repeated text and the illustrations that support it. Children also have an opportunity to practice prediction, as on each page, they will wonder who is at the door.

*Papa, Please Get the Moon for Me* (Carle, 1986). This is a story about a father and his daughter, Monica. Monica asks her father to get the moon for her. He obliges by getting a very long ladder. In the illustrations, it appears that he has in fact climbed to the moon. He gives her a moon that she plays with until it disappears. She keeps watching the sky until a new moon appears. As in other stories in this section, a simple plot has been embellished. (While it is tangential to the theme of imagination, after reading this book, children may want to explore the moon's cycle.)

*The Alphabet From Z to A* (Viorst, 1994). While there are many imaginative alphabet books you might select, we chose Viorst's. This is a very sophisticated book in both illustrations and text related to each letter. It

begins with Z and shares simple words like *zip*, *zap*, and *zero*. Then Viorst includes *xylophone* and wonders why it does not begin with *z*. There are multiple items in each illustration that begin with the letters that are not mentioned in the text. (Viorst lists them at the back of the book.) This fascinating book invites readers to consider alternative ways to create alphabet books; additionally, it encourages children to reflect on interesting spellings of words.

## Vocabulary Extensions

For this, children can create individual posters that share the most interesting vocabulary words used by Kellogg. Students may also compare vocabulary used in different Kellogg texts, or they may discover words he uses across texts. Figure 3.6 showcases several interesting vocabulary words we discovered in Kellogg's books.

Once students have collected words, they can work with a partner and find ways in which the words are alike or different. For instance, children might group *outsmarting, admiration, inspiration*, and *exaggerated* together, as they all relate to being smart or creative. Or they might put *shrieked, clamor, boisterous*, and *frolicking* together because they describe how things are loud. As children group and regroup words they begin to understand them more fully and in more subtle ways.

## VOCABULARY WORD INVESTIGATIONS

| | | | |
|---|---|---|---|
| shrieked | outsmarting | exaggerated | flickering |
| horrified | ambushed | frolicking | urged |
| clamor | inspiration | mousy | foolish |
| simmered | admiration | dubbed | |
| victims | boisterous | threatened | |

FIGURE 3.6: Vocabulary word investigations—Steven Kellogg's books

## Fluency

Second grade typically marks a turning point at which students move beyond word-by-word reading and develop fluency, allowing them read words in groups and have more expression in their reading. One way to help students develop fluency is by having them read multiple books by the same author. We have provided numerous books by Steven Kellogg, and there are many more that support students in becoming more fluent readers. There are also two book series that we believe tie in to the theme of imagination, are interesting to second graders, and support fluency development.

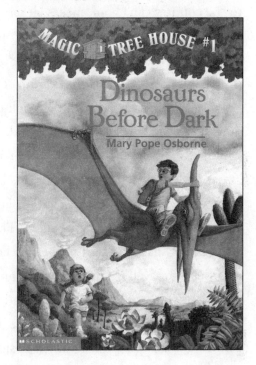

The Magic Tree House Series (Osborne, Scholastic) provides students with adventures. They may be whisked off to Japan to meet samurai warriors or they may find themselves in the time of dinosaurs. In each book, Jack and Annie participate in an adventure that sparks children's imaginations and provides them with scientific and historical facts. Each book is about 70 pages in length, is arranged in chapters, and has much picture support throughout. Each book is numbered and many children will want to start with the first and move through the entire series in order. (There are more than 30 books in this series.)

Black Lagoon Adventures (Thaler, Scholastic) centers on school events such as field days or science fairs. Each story is humorous and there are questions, vocabulary investigations, and riddles throughout. The text is easy to read and there are illustrations on each page to support students as they tackle longer texts. (There are about ten stories in this series.)

## Visual Literacy Extensions

One way to explore visual literacy with students was already mentioned in the author/illustrator section of this chapter. In a careful study of Steven Kellogg's illustrations, students will come to see how much his illustrations are like comics. Each illustration is filled with detail, many depict movement, and some incorporate text. Students may also notice Kellogg's own dog in many of his books. His characters often resemble one another from book to book. Many of his books also feature snakes. As children explore Kellogg's books, they will discover more detail about his artistic style.

We also spent time comparing Sendak's *Where the Wild Things Are* with Kellogg's *Pecos Bill*. We noticed that Sendak and Kellogg both enlarge their illustrations to fill an entire page when the action explodes. Children will notice that illustrations take less space and are more confined when the story is more descriptive or quiet in action.

For a second visual literacy exploration, we chose *Round Trip* (Jonas, 1983). Jonas writes and illustrates a trip to the city and then back home to the country. The book makes clever use of black-and-white illustrations. The trip to the city, which runs from the beginning of the book to the end, features black as the dominant color. For the return trip, children turn the book upside down and read from beginning to end, with white now the dominant color. Children will be amazed when they first encounter this book. They will scrutinize these illustrations as they discover Jonas's talent in creating them. This book also offers a sharp contrast to the rich colors and detail used by Kellogg in his illustrations. You may want your students to try illustrating in the

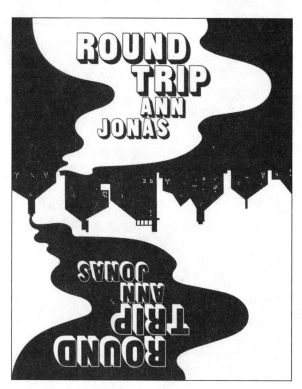

manner of Jonas, although this will be no easy task as the top and bottom of the illustration must connect and, as the page is turned upside down, remain recognizable.

## Connections to Technology
### Focusing on Author Steven Kellogg

There are two good Web sites for extending the study of Kellogg through technology. There is Kellogg's Web site (www.stevenkellogg.com), where children can learn more about Kellogg as a writer and illustrator. The Reading is Fundamental Web site (www.rif.org/art/illustrators/kellogg.mspx) offers information about Kellogg as well, including an interview with the author-illustrator.

### Tall Tale Exploration

For further exploring tall tales try the American Folklore Web site (www.americanfolklore.net/tt.html), which offers information about tall tales and the major characters. So, for instance, children can learn about Paul Bunyan and his blue ox, and the many tales about them. Another Web site, 42explore (http://42explore.com/talltale.htm), provides information to teachers about thematic instruction. This site features many resources for a tall-tale unit, including sites to further explore details about tall-tale characters. The site also provides activities for students related to tall tales, such as writing a tall-tale or comparing characters.

At Animated Tall Tales (www.animatedtalltales.com), we found 14 Paul Bunyan tales that are animated and have audio support, which we're sure children would enjoy. At Terrifically Tall Tales (www.manning.k12.ia.us/Elementary/teachers/talltales/index.html), Manning Community School shares its Internet project centered on the tall tales written and illustrated by Steven Kellogg. Students can explore projects completed by other students.

## Snake Exploration

There are many sites that look closely at snakes. We have provided several that students will enjoy and learn from.

- **42explore.com/snake.htm** This site has information about snakes and provides links to other sites that were created by students.
- **www.enchantedlearning.com/subjects/reptile/snakes/printouts.shtml** This site has a variety of snake information and detailed drawings. When students click on a specific snake, they are taken to a labeled printout of the snake with more information.
- **kids.nationalgeographic.com** Students can click on a photo of a snake and view additional information. There are stories about experts who work with snakes.
- **pbskids.org/dragonflytv/show/snakes.html** Here your students can view a video of two girls exploring snakes.
- **www.sandiegozoo.org/kids/animal_ball_python.htm** Students learn about a ball python and how it survived an illness.
- **www.rattlesnakes.com** This site is the home of the American International Rattlesnake Museum. There are photos and information about rattlesnakes.

## Literacy Activities

The ReadWriteThink site (www.readwritethink.org) has two activities that we thought strongly connected to this exploration. Sequencing: A Strategy to Succeed at Reading Comprehension uses Kellogg's *Paul Bunyan* as an instructional text. Students create a timeline sequence of Bunyan's adventures. The lesson offers a complete lesson plan, a research article to support the activity, and online resource materials. Thundering Tall Tales: Using Read-Aloud as a Springboard to Writing helps children understand the elements of a tall tale and supports them in using the element as they write their own tall tale.

# Connections to Second-Grade Literacy Standards

In this section we list several of the national and state standards that are targeted through the core reading and extended reading and writing extensions described in this chapter. We have shortened the full descriptions of the standards. The full descriptions for national standards are available on the International Reading Association (www.reading.org) and National Council of Teachers of English (www.ncte.org) Web sites. State standards are available on state department of education Web sites.

## International Reading Association and National Council of Teachers of English Literacy Standards

**Standard 1.** Students read a wide range of print and nonprint texts to build understanding of texts. These texts are fiction and nonfiction.

**Standard 3.** Students apply a wide range of strategies to comprehend, interpret, evaluate, and appreciate texts.

**Standard 4.** Students adjust their use of spoken, written, and visual language to communicate effectively.

**Standard 5.** Students use a wide variety of strategies as they write and use different writing process elements.

**Standard 6.** Students apply knowledge of language structure, language conventions, media techniques, figurative language, and genre to create, critique, and discuss print and non-print texts.

**Standard 7.** Students conduct research on issues and interests.

**Standard 8.** Students use technological and information resources to gather information.

**Standard 9.** Students develop an understanding of diversity in language use.

**Standard 11.** Students participate as knowledgeable, reflective, creative, and critical members of literacy communities.

**Standard 12.** Students use spoken, written, and visual language to accomplish their own purposes.

## New York State Language Arts Standards for Second Grade

You can address your state standards through the use and extension of your core reading program. Teachers are most familiar with their state standards and how those standards connect to their language arts curricula. In Chapter Two, we explored California's state language arts standards for first grade. In this chapter, we visit the language arts standards from New York (www.emsc.nysed.gov/ciai/ela/elastandards/elamap.html). New York has four major standards for grades 2 through 4 as noted in their 2005 standards revision. These are as follows:

1.  Students will read, write, listen, and speak for information and understanding.
2.  Students will read, write, listen, and speak for literary response and expression.
3.  Students will read, write, listen, and speak for critical analysis and evaluation.
4.  Students will read, write, listen, and speak for social interaction.

The state then provides further details for each grade under the major categories of reading, writing, listening, and speaking. We list the standards under these categories that the core reading selection and extensions address directly.

### Reading

Students will read, write, listen, and speak for information and understanding.

- Read informational text and collect and interpret data
- Compare and contrast information from two different sources

Students will read, write, listen, and speak for literary response and expression.

- Read print-based and electronic texts
- Recognize differences among genres
- Relate characters in literature to their own lives
- Make predictions and draw conclusions
- Use specific evidence from stories to describe characters or describe a sequence of events

Students will read, write, listen, and speak for critical analysis and evaluation.

- Compare characters in literary work

Students will read, write, listen, and speak for social interaction.

- Share reading experiences
- Recognize the types of language, including formal and informal vocabulary

### Writing

Students will read, write, listen, and speak for information and understanding.

- Connect personal experiences to new information

Students will read, write, listen, and speak for literary response and expression.

- Develop an original literary text
- Create clear, well-organized responses to stories
- Create imaginative stories
- Use personal experience to stimulate writing
- Use a computer to create, research, and interpret literary texts

Students will read, write, listen, and speak for critical analysis and evaluation.

- Use prewriting
- Use relevant examples to support ideas
- Analyze an author's work
- Use effective vocabulary

Students will read, write, listen, and speak for social interaction.

- Share the process of writing with peers
- Use language, including formal and informal vocabulary, that is appropriate to the genre

## Listening

Students will read, write, listen, and speak for information and understanding.

- Identify essential details
- Determine a sequence
- Identify main ideas

Students will read, write, listen, and speak for literary response and expression.

- Identify elements of character, plot, and setting
- Connect literary texts to previous life experiences

Students will read, write, listen, and speak for critical analysis and evaluation.

- Form a personal opinion of the quality of texts

Students will read, write, listen, and speak for social interaction.

- Listen to narratives read aloud

## Speaking

Students will read, write, listen, and speak for information and understanding.

- Express an opinion
- Ask questions

Students will read, write, listen, and speak for literary response and expression.

- Present original work to classmates
- Describe characters
- Ask questions to clarify text

Students will read, write, listen, and speak for critical analysis and evaluation.

- Explain the reasons for a character's actions
- Discuss the impact of illustrations
- Use personal experience to analyze new ideas
- Take turns in a group

Students will read, write, listen, and speak for social interaction.

- Avoid interrupting in conversation

Within each of these broad standards are lists of specific skills that students are expected to acquire during second grade. For reading, these include decoding facility, print awareness that includes knowing about the author, fluency, vocabulary, comprehension strategies with which students compare story plot and characters, and motivation. In writing, students are expected to write in response to text, write original text, use conventions, and share writing with others. Speaking and listening skills cluster around communicating effectively and listening attentively.

Through combining both the core reading program selection and an extended literature-based curriculum, students meet the expectations of national and state standards. Moreover, students have time and opportunities to extend their learning and gain knowledge more thoroughly so that they can apply it appropriately. And, most important, students are engaged in and motivated by reading and writing.

# CHAPTER 4

# *T*hird-Grade Possibilities

*D*o you remember when Despereaux was in the dungeon, cupped in Gregory the *jailer's hand, whispering a story in the old man's ear? I would like it very much if you thought of me as the mouse telling you a story, this story, with the whole of my heart, whispering it in your ear in order to save myself from the darkness, and to save you from the darkness too. "Stories are light," Gregory the jailer told Despereaux. Reader, I hope you have found some light here.*

—Kate DiCamillo, *The Tale of Despereaux*

To explore third-grade possibilities and to connect literature-based reading with core program expectations, we chose the Houghton Mifflin basal series (Houghton Mifflin, 2005) and, as theme three, Incredible Stories. In this chapter we will discuss many reading and questioning strategies for you to consider as you develop your reading program within your third-grade classroom as well as make connections to the literature-based curricula. As with the first- and second-grade explorations, this chapter will also explore multiple ways to extend and enhance the core reading program by offering choice to students and highlighting reading practices that engage and meet the needs of a variety of readers in the classroom.

## The Core Reading Program

The central theme for the core program and for this chapter is Incredible Stories. This theme focuses on the genre of fantasy and investigates many connections between fantasy and reality. Within this theme there are four major text selections. These include *Dogzilla* (Pilkey, 1993), *The Mysterious Giant of Barletta* (dePaola, 1984), *Raising Dragons* (Nolen, 1998), and *The Garden of Abdul Gasazi* (Van Allsburg, 1979). All of the titles are from the fantasy genre and range from folktales to modern fantasy. We chose *Dogzilla* and *The Garden of Abdul Gasazi* as our cornerstone texts. We will use *Dogzilla* to highlight the core reading expectations and *The Garden of Abdul Gasazi* to feature an in-depth author study of Chris Van Allsburg, whose many books offer possibilities for extending and understanding the fantasy genre.

*Dogzilla* is the first reading selection and sets the tone for thinking about Incredible Stories, the corresponding theme. The core reading program has many specific skills and strategies it addresses with this text. The list that follows includes a description of what is expected for student engagement with this text as teachers and readers follow the core reading program.

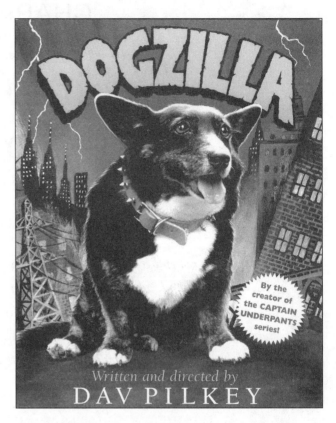

## Comprehension

- Attend to the differences between fantasy and realism
- Evaluate the effectiveness of the author in creating a fantastical story; students should think about the selection they are reading and evaluate their personal responses
- Set a purpose for reading as they consider the fantasy genre and pay particular attention to those elements that can happen in real life and those that can't
- Make inferences throughout the reading of the story
- Read smaller passages to practice fluency

## Word Knowledge
### Decoding
- Focus on plurals with words ending in *f* and *fe*
### Phonics Review
- Practice and learn the vowel sounds in *clown/lawn*
### Vocabulary
- Use context clues to learn the meaning of unknown words
### Spelling
- Practice and learn the vowel sounds in *clown/lawn*

## Fluency

- Read and reread text passages with a partner

## Writing

- Participate in a writer's workshop to create a story and work through five phases of the writing process: prewriting, drafting, revising, editing, proofreading, and publishing
- Focus their efforts on ideas, conventions, and presentation as part of their work with the 6 Traits; as students work through their story they are asked to pay attention to and add details to their story
- Work on multiple graphic organizers to think about and organize writing throughout the writing process
- Consider developing plot, characters, and setting
- Become familiar with journal writing and use a journal as a way to develop and think about ideas for a story
- Practice using possessive nouns
- Present an illustration

There are many activities and teaching strategies created around the core text and theme. As with many core programs, students receive small-group instruction with texts that correspond with the theme and more specifically connect to the reading selection. There are *many* aspects to this core reading program, and there is no need to utilize every activity that is offered; rather, you can choose those activities that meet the needs of all students and those that help students engage in various reading practices. There are numerous worksheets that accompany every skill lesson presented within the theme. We recommend moving away from the worksheets and guiding students into utilizing a journal to demonstrate their new understandings, rather than fill in the predetermined answers on the worksheets.

In the following section we offer possible alternatives for launching the core program theme and interacting with the core reading selection. We also offer ideas on how to teach students through the use of engaging questioning strategies that move readers beyond the literal understanding and allow the flow of the story to be maintained.

## Launching the Theme

Rather than launching into a fantasy genre investigation by defining the genre for the students, it is more engaging to have students help create the criteria for selection and evaluation of the genre.

Allowing students the opportunity to highlight what they already know about the genre deepens their understanding of the variety of texts that might be included. This introduction might take an extra day but helps with the core reading program target skill, which is to evaluate fantasy stories. If students are to evaluate the genre, they first need to understand what the genre is.

To launch the theme, ask your students to bring in their favorite fantasy books. You'll be able to see how much your students already know about the fantasy genre by observing the titles they bring in. Ask why they brought in the selection they did. Ask students what makes it fantasy. Make note of any selections that push the boundaries, like poetry or texts that use the informational genre structure but are fantasy, such as *The Discovery of Dragons* (Base, 1996). Then review those fantasy titles read previously in the school year. Have students create an example/non-example T-chart to list those that could be considered fantasy and those that might not. Review books like *Lilly's Purple Plastic Purse* (Henkes,1996) and ask why some see the book as fantasy and others consider it realistic fiction. (This example assumes that students are familiar with realistic fiction.) Then read aloud *Dogzilla*, the introductory story within the core program, and see how that introduces the genre as well.

After reviewing student selections, you might begin a list of criteria and create a "Possible Characteristics of Fantasy" chart to which your students can refer. After the chart is complete you might ask your students what they like about the books they brought in and begin a "Criteria for Evaluation" chart. Students become empowered and engage with the selections and independent reading choices at a deeper level if they have a beginning understanding about the genre. Once students have created criteria for defining and evaluating, you can add to this list by drawing from your own knowledge of fantasy or from lists found in many children's literature textbooks or Web sites.

Once your students understand the fantasy genre, you can then return to the core program and engage with the first and subsequent core program reading selections that introduce the theme. When at all possible, we recommend obtaining a hardcover copy of the reading selections, as a hard cover has many peritextual elements that the selection in the anthology does not. Peritextual information includes all the parts of a book besides the actual text and illustrations, including the cover, end pages, jacket, inside and back jacket information, author's notes, dedication, and copyright information. The peritextual elements contain a great deal of information about a text and with close reading can provide students with background information to engage with the text at a much deeper level. It is interesting to compare these different editions with students. You might begin with the anthology, then look at a paperback, a library version, and finally a hardcover copy with a jacket. Students begin to see the changes that were made to the texts for monetary as well as space considerations. The hardcover can be made available to students to preview and read as they analyze the peritextual information. You may also decide to read this hardcover copy as a read-aloud or just read the peritextual information to set the stage for independent or paired reading.

Another way to set the stage for reading is to ask children to look at the cover and predict what they think will happen in the story. This reading practice asks students to attend to the unknown in a story, rather than to attend to what is known (Serafini & Youngs, in press). Instead, we suggest asking children what they notice on the cover, as this practice asks students to attend to what is there. Once students point out what they notice, you can ask how that information might impact their understanding of the text.

After you have introduced the genre and attended to the peritextual information in *Dogzilla*, you may invite your students to pair-read the selection, read it independently, read it in small groups, or read it in small groups with your support. We recommend this practice of independent reading, as it allows readers to have an opportunity to formulate their own ideas and questions about the text. The core program for *Dogzilla* asks three and four questions a page! Many of the questions are at the literal level, break the flow of the story, and are at times very leading. If students do not read the selection for themselves first, they will all be led to think about the text in the same way, especially if they are guided by explicit questioning. We are not saying not to follow the core reading guidelines and questioning; we are just recommending that you allow students time with the text to formulate their own ideas first, then come back to the questions and vocabulary focus afterward. Students will be more engaged and might offer new and interesting insights about the story.

You might also give your students a pack of sticky notes to mark places of interest or confusion, or to mark new and interesting words. On the whiteboard or chalkboard, record, review, and model the target strategies; for this text the target strategy is to evaluate and attend to the differences between fantasy and realism. You might allow students to read and mark places where they are using the evaluation strategy and then mark evidence in the text and illustrations of the difference between fantasy and realism. Invite your students to consider how the author includes both and how that impacts the meaning of the story. You might also extend this reading by asking your students to attend to literary and visual elements and think about which elements are prominent within the fantasy genre.

After students engage with the text, you might follow the more explicit suggestions in the teacher's edition. Allowing students to engage with the text first empowers them to think about the text based on their own literate and personal experiences, rather than allowing the program to guide their thinking. Students will still be successful with reading because teachers follow the recommendations in the program. The difference is that students have analyzed the genre and/or text selection and have come to their own conclusions first. Building on this practice demonstrates your faith in your students as accomplished readers.

## Rethinking Questioning

In this section, we help readers and teachers move beyond the literal level in their questioning strategies. As you read through the core program, you will notice that the teachers' edition is replete with questions. There are 30 questions for *Dogzilla*—a short picture book— and most of them are at the literal level. Every question has a predetermined answer the core reading program authors consider to be the best or most logical. These answers do not allow young readers the freedom to explore many response opportunities, as teachers often look for answers that are just like or close to those given in the margins. We recommend that you evaluate the kinds of questions that are asked and make decisions as to which are important. Indeed, many of the questions might become unnecessary as students address these same ideas in their initial reading of and responding to the text.

First and foremost, there are too many questions to answer in the reading of the text. They break the flow. Also, many are leading questions, for example, *Why do you think the mice are terrified of Dogzilla?* Allow students to come to their own conclusions as to the mice's demeanor. As we have explained in previous chapters and selections, the authors provide more opportunities than you might ever need to interact with the text, and the same holds true with the questions. You might even consider having your students create questions as well. Consider the following notions about questions when reading and sharing a book with students and when evaluating core reading program questions:

- How often do students ask questions?
- What is the ratio of talk between teacher and students?
- Analyze questions and limit questions to those that lead to inquiry; some comprehension check-up questions, for example, are okay as they support basic understanding.
- Allow children to read first and formulate their own questions and ideas, then come back for whole-group discussion.
- Turn some questions into statements.
- Don't ask questions to which students already know the answers.
  (Serafini & Giorgis, 2003)

The main point of any reading program is to help children comprehend the text, not to adhere blindly to the program itself. Any program is just an avenue to meaning. Analyze the program, get to know your students, and then make decisions that best meet the needs of all your readers.

# The Extended Literacy Curriculum

*The Garden of Abdul Gasazi*, the third reading selection in the core program, is a wonderful entrance into the world of fantasy. It offers readers examples to consider as they investigate fantasy selections. To begin our extended investigation, students can engage in an in-depth study of author and illustrator Chris Van Allsburg. For this unit of study we can divide the unit into three parts: exposure, exploration, and experimentation. We shall describe each below.

## Exposure to Chris Van Allsburg Books

Students will become familiar with all the Chris Van Allsburg books brought into the class for reading and discussion. Some titles will be reserved for think-aloud and discussion.

### Books Written by Chris Van Allsburg

*Bad Day at Riverbend*

*Ben's Dream*

*The Garden of Abdul Gasazi*

*Jumanji*

*Just a Dream*

*The Mysteries of Harris Burdick*

*The Polar Express*

*Probuditi!*

*The Stranger*

*The Sweetest Fig*

*Two Bad Ants*

*The Polar Express*

*The Widow's Broom*

*The Wreck of the Zephyr*

*The Wretched Stone*

*Zathura*

*The Z Was Zapped*

*The Garden of Abdul Gasazi* is a great book to begin the investigation, as it was Van Allsburg's very first book. You can begin and end the investigation with a read-aloud of this book to see what readers have learned about Van Allsburg, his writing and illustrations, and the fantasy genre in general, and how these elements impact their interpretations of this picture book.

During this phase students will also begin to look for patterns, similarities, and differences within his books (see Figure 4.1 for an example chart) and begin to discuss with each other ideas and interpretations about his writing and illustrations.

You might introduce charts (see Figure 4.2) to record interesting information about Van Allsburg as well as students' interpretations and ideas about his books. Students can add to the charts as new ideas develop during their discussions of the texts. You might also create an inde-

| BOOK | TEXT | ILLUSTRATIONS | SIMILARITIES TO OTHER BOOKS | DIFFERENCES |
|---|---|---|---|---|
| *Two Bad Ants* | Told from third person but from an ant's point of view | Colored drawings bring the story to life, uses lines to create movement | Uses a variety of perspectives; mysterious tone; ants go on an adventure, learn a lesson | Color illustrations; two ants get into trouble; everyday objects are made to be fantastic because they are seen from the ant's point of view |
| *Probuditi!* | Mysterious third person tells a story | Uses burnt sienna to set the tone of the setting and to portray extreme heat | Uses many perspectives; keeps you wondering until the end | Burnt sienna illustrations; set in the 1940s; about magic, that in the end it wasn't magic after all |
| *Jumanji* | Third person tells the story; excitement created through the story and plot | Black-and-white pencil drawings create mysterious mood | Uses many perspectives; sets up the end of the book with a twist | Black-and-white game board comes to life; animals and people seem so real |

FIGURE 4.1: Comparison Chart for Van Allsburg Books

| VAN ALLSBURG INFORMATION | IDEAS, CONNECTIONS, AND QUESTIONS |
|---|---|
| Born in Grand Rapids, Michigan | His books are very mysterious and they leave you hanging in the end; you really wonder what will happen. |
| Houses on the cover of *Polar Express* were like those in his own neighborhood growing up. | The stories are told through the illustrations as much as the text. You need to analyze both to understand his stories. |
| He began his art career at the University of Michigan, where he found that he liked to create sculptures, and continued on at the Rhode Island School of Design. | His stories are centered around children having a grand adventure. In *Probuditi!* he tricks us, as we believe something magical will happen, but find out it was just the sister tricking the brother . . . that was very clever. |
| His wife, Lisa, helped him to get published. She used his drawings in the elementary school art classes she taught. | Does he draw first or write first? Do his illustrations make him change the tex,t and does the text enhance his drawings? |

FIGURE 4.2: Van Allsburg charts

pendent author center. On this table you can set up computers with access to Van Allsburg's very interactive Web site (www.chrisvanallsburg.com/home.html). In this center you might include all the books available for independent reading, and pictures of his paintings and sculptures for students to become familiar with as well. The purpose of this first phase is simply for children to get exposed to the author and his works so they have background knowledge to further their understandings in the exploration phase.

## Exploration of Van Allsburg as Writer and Illustrator

During this phase, students discover Van Allsburg's writing and illustrations and the interplay between the two, as well as learn about Van Allsburg to enhance their reading and understanding of his books. Students begin to explore the way he writes and draws. They make comparisons to other books, apply facts and details of his life to their overall understanding, and discuss with one another the influence this knowledge of him as an author has on comprehension. In this phase, students add to the charts they began in the exposure phase.

On the wall behind the table you might create an "Interesting Words of Chris Van Allsburg" word wall and allow students to add to it as they read his texts. Next to the word wall you might post a series of pictures that act as examples of all the different perspectives he uses in his illustrations. Analysis of both words and illustrations enables children to understand the interplay between the two elements.

You can hang graffiti boards (Serafini, 2004) on a wall or on a door and have students draw their interpretations of the books they read, much like a sketch-to-stretch activity. Venn diagrams of *Zathura* and *Jumanji* could also be used to discuss the differences and similarities between the two texts. Finally, students could read *The Polar Express* and *Jumanji*, then watch the movies and compare. Students can discuss what happens when a story moves across modes.

When text and 32 illustrations turn into moving images, what happens? What can text and illustrations do that the movie cannot, and what can the movie do that text and still images cannot? We are usually quick to judge that the book was better than the movie. Rather then simply agree with the statement, have children engage in an analysis of the two different modes. This investigation can enhance comprehension as students read with a critical eye and compare the differences between modes.

To complete the exploration phase, students can respond to the various books in a response log, keep a notebook filled with information on Van Allsburg, and then create comparison charts to explore various literary and visual elements as well as personal responses to his books. Students might enjoy writing a letter to Van Allsburg as they share their thoughts and ideas on their favorite books. These titles could also be shared with reading buddies in the lower grades. As students gain a greater appreciation for Van Allsburg and the fantasy genre, they might try out his style of writing during the experimentation phase.

## Experimentation With Van Allsburg's Style

During the experimentation phase, students can try to emulate Van Allsburg's style by writing stories that are mysterious and told through image as well as text. Students can choose one of his books as a mentor text and then create their own story following the book's structure, plot, and setting, or create characters like the ones in the text. Students become engaged in this kind of writing, as they've come to know so much about Van Allsburg and feel empowered to tell a story through both images and text.

Another possibility for experimentation within this unit would be some of the various writing activities posted on Van Allsburg's Web site. For example, students might partake in the *Mysteries of Harris Burdick* writing contest. You could print the instructions and make this contest available to all of those who are interested. The possibilities are truly endless, as Van Allsburg makes a wonderful fantasy writing teacher. At the end of the unit, students share Van Allsburg's writing with other classes or have a celebration to which parents and friends are invited to listen to the mysterious stories being read. If you are really adventurous, you could arrange a campfire and have students read their stories around it, as the mood of the campfire would be appropriate for the mysterious stories being told.

## Reading Connections

### Other Possible Units of Study

Beyond the selections for the author study, there are many other ways to extend and organize for investigating fantasy selections. For example, there are many subgenres of fantasy to investigate, such as animal fantasy, horror or the supernatural, fairy tale variants, quest fantasy, extraordinary worlds, characters with exceptional traits, animated object or toy fantasy, time-travel fantasy, comic fantasy, high fantasy, and science fiction. You might choose one of the subgenres to explore, and collect several titles for the students to select and read. Then, as a class, create comparison charts and have students independently or in pairs read various titles and respond in reader response logs.

Animal fantasy is a favorite with young readers, and many of the titles in the core reading program fall under this subgenre, so it seems a natural extension for this exploration. In animal fantasy, animals take on a variety of characteristics: They might act like humans and speak with humans, or they might dress like humans but still live in an all-animal world. Research has uncovered four types of animal fantasy (Anderson, 2006). Type I is anthropomorphic animals (animals with human characteristics) in an all-animal world, such as *Sylvester and the Magic Pebble* (Steig, 1969) and *Chrysanthemum* (Henkes, 1991). Type II is anthropomorphic animals coexisting with humans, such as in *Charlotte's Web* (White, 1952) and *The Tale of Despereaux: Being the Story of a Mouse, a Princess, Some Soup, and a Spool of Thread* (DiCamillo, 2003). Type III is talking animals in natural habitats, such as *The Tale of Peter Rabbit* (Potter, 1999). And Type IV is realistic animals with human thinking ability, as in *The Incredible Journey* (Burnford, 1961). You may want to introduce children to the variety of animal fantasy that exists and analyze the types of books and their personal responses to each. In small groups, students could explore one type of animal fantasy and then make comparisons to the other types; in pairs, students could read selections and you could do read-alouds of a variety of titles.

Children's books to explore for each fantasy type include the following:

## Type I

Falconer, I. *Olivia*

Henkes, K. *Chrysanthemum*

Lobel, A. *Frog and Toad Are Friends*

Rohmann, E. *My Friend Rabbit*

Steig, W. *Dominic*

## Type II

Cronin, D. *Click, Clack, Moo: Cows That Type*

Henkes, K. *Kitten's First Full Moon*

Howe, D., & Howe, J. *Bunnicula: A Rabbit-Tale of Mystery*

Kotzwinkle, W., & Murray, G. *Walter the Farting Dog*

Rylant, C. *Henry and Mudge and the Happy Cat*

Teague, M. *Dear Mrs. LaRue: Letters from Obedience School*

White, E. B. *Charlotte's Web*

Willems, M. *Don't Let the Pigeon Drive the Bus*

## Type III

Potter, B. *The Tale of Peter Rabbit*

Cannon, J. *Stellaluna*

Cannon, J. *Verdi*

Carle, E. *The Very Hungry Caterpillar*

Lionni, L. *Frederick*

**Type IV**

Burnford, S. *The Incredible Journey*
London, J. *The Call of the Wild*
George, J. C. *Julie's Wolf Pack*

As a whole-class read-aloud, teachers could begin with *The Tale of Despereaux* and use it as a mentor text to explore the fantasy genre together. This story is more complex than the picture books and might need to be read aloud. *The Tale of Despereaux* is a story about a mouse that does not fit into the mouse world and learns that he can read one day. He happens upon a fairy tale where the knight saves the princess in distress. Despereaux reads a quest fantasy and then falls in love with the princess in the castle in which he lives. The story is told in four parts as the narrator tells the story of the mouse, Despereaux, a rat named Roscuro, and a servant girl named Miggery Sow. The fourth section of the book brings all the stories together, and the fate of all the characters is learned. It is a wonderful fantasy story and one that can be explored as readers

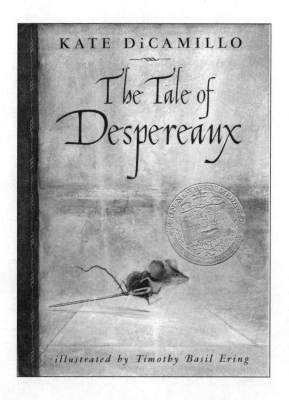

attend to the genre elements—real and fantastical—and evaluate the quality of the story.

The second exploration, *The Three Pigs* by David Wiesner (2001), is an escaping-reality theme in which all the characters leave some problem in the realistic world and escape into a fantasy world. In this story, the pigs' reality is really fantasy and they escape to many other fantasy worlds. This story begins just like the traditional

"Three Little Pigs": The wolf comes to visit and he huffs and he puffs, but on his last puff he blows the pigs right out of the story and into another fantasy world, one that is wedged between other stories, as illustrated by the expanse of white space on the page spreads. The pigs journey in and out of other fantasy stories until they decide to return home, and the book ends much like the traditional one except that they bring home some storybook characters they met along the way.

As an interesting study, try comparing *The Three Pigs* to *Where the Wild Things Are* (Sendak, 1991). You could compare how characters deal with their problems and how fantasy is used to help the characters cope. Readers could again look at the core target skill of comparing reality and fantasy. In Sendak's story, there is a real blend: The main character has a problem in the real world and goes to some fantastical place to escape. Again, a chart is a helpful way to organize and record readers' ideas on the target skill as they identify reality and fantasy elements (see Figure 4.3 for an example).

| FANTASY | | How does fantasy help the character(s) deal with problems? | | REALITY | |
|---|---|---|---|---|---|
| *Wild Things* | *Three Pigs* | *Wild Things* | *Three Pigs* | *Wild Things* | *Three Pigs* |
| He leaves room to go to where the wild things are | Characters are fantasy | He feels better when he is in control | They escape death | Max causes mischief | The traditional tale is reality |
| He becomes king of wild things and controls them | They escape death by going to other stories | He tells them to stop as he becomes the one in charge | They meet interesting characters | Gets in trouble with mom | The pigs try to build their houses |
| There is a wild rumpus | They meet other fantasy characters | He has a wild rumpus | Pigs take charge of their own reality | He is sent to his room without supper | The wolf tries to eat them |
| He travels over a year to get home | They leave one fantasy world to enter another | He calms down after the rumpus is over and he returns home | They save other characters from boredom and slaying | His supper is in his room and still hot | The wolf huffs and puffs and blows the house in |

FIGURE 4.3: Fantasy/reality T-chart for *The Three Pigs* and *Where the Wild Things Are*

Readers might also note how fantasy as escaping reality relates to their own lives and their desires to escape to imaginary worlds when they feel bored or scared.

## Other "Escaping Reality" Titles

Juster, N. *The Hello Goodbye Window*

Lehman, B. *The Red Book*

Ringgold, F. *Tar Beach*

Van Allsburg, C. *Just a Dream*

Wiesner, D. *Flotsam*

As you organize for your reading block, you can easily implement literature study groups (Peterson & Eeds, 2007) that are formed based on student interest in a fantasy chapter book or picture book. You could add a 20-minute block of reading time to include circle, seat, center, or literature study. In this way, students meet in strategy groups or guided-reading groups, according to their reading ability, as well as meet in groups that match their interests, allowing them to discuss literature with their peers, regardless of ability.

Students read and discuss these titles each week. Depending on scheduling demands and the needs of students, groups can meet with you once, twice, or three times a week. Students share their insights and you scaffold students in discussing literature at an in-depth level. Student input helps balance the reading curriculum. Students choose the fantasy titles they will discuss. The following is a list of good fantasy titles for discussion for third grade.

Applegate, K. A. *The Encounter* (Animorphs #3)

Babbit, N. *Tuck Everlasting*

Conrad, P. *Stonewords*

Coville, B. *Into the Land of the Unicorns*

Dahl, R. *The BFG*

Dahl, R. *Matilda*

Fleischmann, S. *The Whipping Boy*

Gormley, B. *Back to the Day Lincoln Was Shot*

Howe, J. *Bunnicula*

Irving, W. *Legend of Sleepy Hollow*

Le Guin, U. K. U. *Catwing's Return*

Lobel, A. *Frog and Toad Are Friends*

Milne, A. A. *Winnie-the-Pooh*

Rylant, C. *The Islander*

Rylant, C. *The Van Gogh Café*

Sachar, L. *Sideways Stories from Wayside School*

Schwartz, A. *Scary Stories to Tell in the Dark*

Scieszka, J. Time Warp Trio series

Selden, G. *The Cricket in Times Square*

Steig, W. *Dominic*

White, E. B. *Charlotte's Web*

Literature study groups enable you and your students to choose the books that you find most intriguing, and your students then benefit from reading and discussing as members of a community of readers.

## Writing Connections

The core program suggests that students create a story. Through this writing activity, students learn about the various aspects of the writing process as well as the writing trait elements. We suggest two writing projects that enhance their understanding of the fantasy genre as well as support their writing of a fantasy piece.

### Fairy Tale Variant

After reading numerous fairy tales and fairy tale variants and attending to how they are structured, students could create one themselves. This writing activity requires students to understand the fantasy genre well. There are numerous ways to approach writing fairy tale variants, but we recommend students change only *one* aspect of a story. This may seem simple, but they soon realize that one literary element impacts the other elements and the story as a whole.

For example, if writers wanted to change the setting of Snow White, they would need to consider a new time and place rather than an English or French countryside long, long ago. As students consider new and interesting settings, they soon realize in their planning that the setting impacts the perspective, plot, characters, mood, and theme. You might create a chart to guide students' thinking about all the changes that would need to take place if they were to change the setting. You might first fill in the chart with an existing fairy tale to model the process and then, independently or in pairs, students could begin to write their own fairy tale variant. To model this process, read the traditional "Snow White: A Tale by the Brothers Grimm" (2004), and then a variant, such as *Snow White in New York* by French (1990). As students consider the various elements in each story (see Figure 4.4), they will soon realize that when Fiona French changed the setting of the tale, it affected the rest of the story.

The following list contains possibilities to consider when creating a fairy tale variant:

- Change the prose style, from old-fashioned to modern language
- Change or add to the details in the plot
- Change a few of the main events in the plot
- Keep a few of the main events but change most of the plot
- Change the setting (time and place); if the setting is changed, it is likely to cause additional changes in characters and details
- Change the point of view
- Change the characters in the story by:
  - Changing their occupation
  - Changing their gender
  - Reversing their roles in the story

| | "Snow White" (Traditional Version) | Snow White in New York by Fiona French |
|---|---|---|
| SETTING | Woods, long ago | New York City, 1920s |
| CHARACTERS | Snow White is kind and good and wears a long dress | Snow White is a singer in a jazz club and wears a flapper dress |
| PLOT | • Evil queen wants to kill her<br>• The seven dwarves save her<br>• The prince kisses her | • Evil stepmother wants her out of New York society, so she sends her to the streets of New York all alone<br>• The seven jazz players save her<br>• Photographer with *Daily Mirror* kisses her |
| ILLUSTRATIONS | Renaissance, romantic | Art deco |

FIGURE 4.4: Snow White comparison chart

- Write a sequel to the original story
- Keep the words of the original story, but change the illustrations (Sipe, 1993a)

**Realistic Fiction to Fantasy**

The second writing activity asks students to take one of their favorite realistic fiction stories and change it into a fantasy story. As students consider how to do this, it is important for them to review the criteria for defining fantasy as well as for evaluating it. As students consider how to change a realistic story into a fantasy one, they attend to the delicate balance of reality and fantasy, think about the criteria for the genre, and attend to literary and visual elements that help to tell a good story. You will certainly need to model how to do this as a whole class first. This could be a great shared-writing activity.

# Extension of the Core Reading Program Theme

To extend the core reading program theme, we have selected books that are grouped together based on techniques used by the author and/or illustrator. Illustrative and textual techniques move the titles beyond the traditional fantasy story into a category called postmodern literature. Each book in this collection is written and illustrated by one person who tells us an amazing story through image and text. At times the illustrations tell more of the story than the text, and at times the illustrations seem to tell a different story from what the text is presenting.

Postmodern picture books can contain a variety of genres, as in *The Jolly Postman or Other People's Letters* (Ahlberg & Ahlberg, 1986); multiple perspectives and a juxtaposition of unrelated images, as in *Voices in the Park* (Browne, 2001); unique treatment of time, as in *Bright and Early Thursday Evening* (Wood, 1996); and irony and ambiguity, as in *The Three Pigs* (Wiesner, 2001). Reading many of these books aloud creates a wonderful atmosphere for discussion, as the ambiguity created in both the text and illustrations allows for numerous interpretations.

To begin the series of read-alouds, we recommend choosing a cornerstone text that encompasses many of the postmodern techniques. We chose *Voices in the Park* by Anthony Browne. This is a book about four people—a mother and her son and a father and his daughter—who go to the park. They each tell their own story and share their own perspective of their day at the park. All of the stories are told simultaneously and much of the story is conveyed through the interplay between text and image. Each voice is separate and complete and there is no transition between the stories.

Children might be confused on the first reading, as the stories are separate but happen at the same time. There are many hidden images that bring meaning to the text. It is up to the reader to bring the four stories together. We recommend taking a few days to read and reread the text and make it available to the class for independent reading. Students will certainly want to talk about Browne's use of gorillas for the main characters, as well as to point to the myriad of visual images. Numerous social issues are addressed in the story. Browne uses class to show a difference between the two families. This is a great book for discussion and for analyzing the power of images.

The following books could be read independently or in pairs and investigated and analyzed more closely in small groups.

*Come Away From the Water, Shirley* (Burningham, 1977) is another great book to explore. This picture book is about a little girl named Shirley who goes to the beach with her parents. Her parents are not paying any attention to Shirley, which is shown through the illustrations. Shirley's parents read the paper and tell her to come away from the water and to stay away from a stray dog, as well as giving her many other parental warnings. Shirley's story is told only through the illustrations, which depict her going on a great pirate adventure with the stray dog and searching for a buried treasure. Each two-page spread contains Shirley's parents on the left with text, and Shirley on the

right having a grand time. Children will engage with this text and certainly will want to investigate the contradiction between text and image.

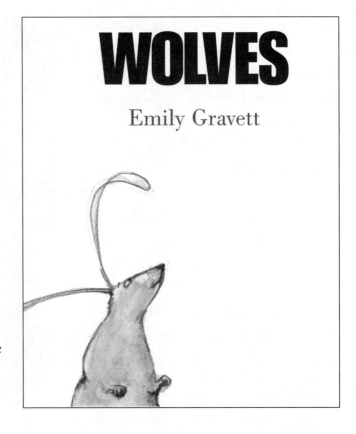

*Wolves* (Gravett, 2006) is a story within a story. The book is written with rabbits, or children who think they're rabbits, as the intended audience! The main character, a rabbit, goes to his local library to check out the book *Wolves*. As he is reading it, the wolf in the story begins to leave the story and get closer and closer to the rabbit until the wolf finally eats the rabbit. Then the author cleverly provides a very humorous alternate ending. True to many postmodern selections, this book includes humorous details in the peritextual information that entice readers to read closely.

These books, as well as those listed below, support the target skills highlighted in the core reading program, but also give students a larger range and experience with a variety of fantasy titles and subgenres. Teachers could engage students in identifying and learning about the various techniques and terminology used, ways to analyze and discuss these texts, and how to make comparisons across titles and with those included in the core program.

## Other Postmodern Picture Book Titles
Ahlberg, J., & Ahlberg, A. *The Jolly Postman or Other People's Letters*
Base, G. *The Discovery of Dragons*
Browne, A. *Changes*
Browne, A. *Willy's Pictures*
Browne, A. *Zoo*
Macauley, D. *Why the Chicken Crossed the Road*
Macauley, D. *Black and White*

Macauley, D. *Shortcut*

Say, A. *Home of the Brave*

Say. A. *Stranger in the Mirror*

Scieszka, J. *The Stinky Cheese Man and Other Fairly Stupid Tales*

Sis, P. *Starry Messenger*

Thompson, C. *Looking for Atlantis*

Van Allsburg, C. *Bad Day at Riverbend*

Wiesner, D. *Tuesday*

Wiesner, D. *The Three Pigs*

Willard, N. *Pish, Posh, Said Hieronymus Bosch*

Wood, A. *Bright and Early Thursday Evening: A Tangled Tale*

## Vocabulary Extensions

We suggested in Chapter Three that students create posters to record interesting and new words found in the Kellogg books. We suggest a similar approach with the Van Allsburg books. As students take note of the kinds of words he uses, they can record these words in a notebook and use them later in their own writing. Students might take note of words used across fantasy titles and put these up on a special fantasy word wall. When students are allowed to add words to the wall, they begin to pay attention to what is up there and how they can contribute. They begin to attend to new and interesting words, either to add to the wall or to use in their own writing. Teachers could also call attention to the verbs used in the fantasy genre and analyze how they move the plot along (see Figure 4.5) and perhaps attend to the endings of words as well.

### POSSIBLE WORD WALL FOR FANTASY GENRE

| | | | |
|---|---|---|---|
| enrolled | punished | floating | explore |
| steals | clawing | entered | huff and puff |
| chases | shattered | poked | blew |
| howls | launches | hopped | |

FIGURE 4.5: Possible word wall for fantasy genre

## Fluency

Through the core program, students are required to read shorter passages to a partner to practice their oral fluency of a few passages. We suggest two other ways to help all readers practice fluency while attending to the fantasy genre. First, students could create and practice with a Readers Theater script. The script could come from one of the stories read or from the variants they wrote. Readers Theater is an engaging way for children to practice fluency and comprehension. It is also a safe and empowering way to practice—students can work on their own or with a partner before performing the reading. Students have numerous experiences with the text and are able to continue to work through a piece until they feel they are ready.

Another way to help children practice fluency is with reading buddies. Students choose and practice reading an easier book that they will read to a kindergartner or a first grader. Students practice reading the text with inflection and passion so they can perform the piece of literature and engage their young reading partners. Young readers will be thrilled with the fantasy selections, and the texts provide great discussion opportunities as well. This is an ideal reading activity for struggling readers, who get to practice with the easier books they present to their reading buddies. You will want to pay careful attention to matching reading buddies to ensure that the older reader is the expert.

## Visual Literacy Extensions

Students can compare and analyze many illustrations found in the variety of fantasy picture books throughout this unit of study. However, without explicit instruction on visual literacy, students may not understand the power of the image to convey meaning. You can learn along with your students as you become more familiar with various design elements. For this fantasy unit of study and with the focus on Chris Van Allsburg and postmodern picture books, we suggest introducing color and point of view for analysis and evaluation. As readers view the books in this genre they attend to variety of color, purposeful hue, and various points of view.

Begin with one book to serve as a mentor text and analyze color and point of view through the use of think-alouds as well as whole-class discussion. As you become familiar and comfortable with these design elements, you can return to the same book and attend to other visual design elements, such as shape, shape placement, line, texture, distance, and framing. For this unit we chose *The Three Pigs* by David Wiesner, which is filled with a variety of design elements that convey much of the meaning of this book.

The colors, hues, and textures of the illustrations guide the reader to understand the various fantasy or literary worlds the three pigs journey into and out of. The book begins traditionally, with the wolf coming to eat the pigs. Wiesner colored the pigs in a cartoonish way with subdued hues and very little texture. However, once the wolf blows the pigs out of the story, they change in texture and color to look very lifelike. Their color continues to change as they go in and out of the different stories. The hard cover of the book is gray, like sticks, the binding is red, like brick, and the endpages are the color of straw. The color scheme shows a variety of tans, pinks, and grays with varying textures to connect with the various stories or *realities* the pigs are a part of.

Wiesner also uses a variety of perspectives to tell the pigs' story. In the beginning he uses panels to show the progression of the story, but once the pigs are outside of the story they actually bump and move the panels of the continuing story. The text continues with the traditional tale, yet the illustrations show that the wolf is very perplexed. As the pigs leave their own story, they fold it up into a paper airplane and fly around on it; the pigs are placed high on the page looking down, portraying a sense of freedom and power. The wolf is wrapped up in the paper airplane, looking down. There is also a moment when one of the pigs looks directly at the reader and says, "I think someone's out there." This perspective draws the reader in and provides evidence of the pigs' reality. *The Three Pigs* provides endless possibilities for discussion and analysis.

## Connections to Technology

### Focus on Author Chris Van Allsburg

There are many Web sites that provide a variety of information about Chris Van Allsburg. Below is a list that will enhance the genre and author study.

- **www.chrisvanallsburg.com** This is the official Chris Van Allsburg Web site. It contains video clips of Van Allsburg speaking on a range of topics. It shows images of his earlier work, and it has a timeline of his publications. This site is great for teachers and students to explore and learn.
- **www.readingrockets.org/books/interviews/vanallsburg** This site features a video interview with Chris Van Allsburg.
- **www.houghtonmifflinbooks.com/features/thepolarexpress** This site features *The Polar Express*, the book and the movie. It shows trailers for the movie and excerpts from the book.
- **falcon.jmu.edu/~ramseyil/allsburg.htm** This is a teacher-resource file; teachers will find a biography, criticism, and ready-to-use lesson plans.
- **www.kidsreads.com/authors/au-van-allsburg-chris.asp** Kids Reads features an interview with Van Allsburg about *Probuditi!* his latest book. It is an exciting interview as he reveals his inspiration, illustrative techniques, and the meaning of the word *probuditi*.

## Multimedia Creations

There are numerous multimedia programs available for classroom use. Kid Pix is a program featured in many school computer labs as well as on classroom computers. This program allows children to explore the mixed media of photography and drawing. Students can download photos and then use the Kid Pix drawing tool to illustrate around the photograph, as Dav Pilkey did in *Dogzilla*. Students might also choose to cut out photos and glue them to a page and illustrate around it as they experiment with photos and illustrations.

## Creating Classroom Blogs

If a school or classroom has a Web site, you can easily begin blogs to which students can post their fantasy stories and other students can post their comments and responses to them. This posting gives students authentic publishing possibilities as well as the opportunity to connect with other fantasy readers around the world. Students can post their fantasy writing pieces and read them aloud for others to listen to as well. Students might also want to videotape their Readers Theater plays or create a play of one of their favorite stories and post these as well.

Lastly, writers in a classroom can begin a fantasy story, create the setting, and then post for other visitors to add to. Much like a circle story, in which everyone in the class adds to the story, this would be online, so many other students would have access to it. Students would be eager to read the new postings each day. Students could even create multiple possibilities for the same stories and propose and create alternate endings. Authentic publications and connections to other cultures can be a very powerful learning tool and can entice reluctant readers to engage with creative texts created online.

# Connections to Third-Grade Literacy Standards

In this section we list the national and state standards that are targeted through the core reading program as well as the extended literacy curriculum suggested in this chapter. As stated previously, the full description of the standards are available on the International Reading Association (www.reading.org) and National Council of Teachers of English (www.ncte.org) Web sites.

**Standard 1.** Students read a wide range of print and nonprint texts to build an understanding of texts. These selections include mostly fiction, classic and contemporary works, and some nonfiction.

**Standard 3.** Students apply a wide range of strategies to comprehend, interpret, evaluate, and appreciate texts.

**Standard 4.** Students adjust their use of spoken, written, and visual language (e.g., conventions, style, vocabulary) to communicate effectively.

**Standard 5.** Students employ a wide range of strategies as they write and use different writing process elements.

**Standard 6.** Students apply knowledge of language structure, language conventions, media techniques, figurative language, and genre to create, critique, and discuss print and non-print texts.

**Standard 8.** Students use a variety of technological and information resources to gather and synthesize information.

**Standard 11.** Students participate as knowledgeable, reflective, creative, and critical members of a variety of literacy communities.

**Standard 12.** Students use spoken, written, and visual language.

## Georgia State English Language Arts Standards for Third Grade

To connect the core program and the extended curriculum to state standards, we chose to align to the Georgia state standards (www.georgiastandards.org/) for third grade. Georgia has newly revised standards and has broken its performance standards down by grade and subject area to address reading, writing, speaking, and listening. Below is a list of the Georgia state standards that the core reading selection and extensions address specifically.

### Reading

The student demonstrates the ability to read orally with speed, accuracy, and expression.

- Applies letter-sound knowledge to decode unknown words quickly and accurately
- Reads familiar text with expression
- Uses self-correction when subsequent reading indicates an earlier misreading within grade-level texts

The student acquires and uses grade-level words to communicate effectively.

- Reads literary and informational texts and incorporates new words into oral and written language
- Identifies the meaning of common idioms and figurative phrases and incorporates them into oral and written language

- Identifies and infers meaning from common root words, common prefixes (e.g., *un-*, *re-*, *dis-*, *in-*) and common suffixes (e.g., *-tion*, *-ous*, *-ly*)
- Determines the meaning of unknown words on the basis of context

The student uses a variety of strategies to gain meaning from grade-level text.

- Reads a variety of texts for information and pleasure
- Makes predictions from text content
- Generates questions to improve comprehension
- Recognizes plot, setting, and character within text, and compares and contrasts these elements between texts
- Makes judgments and inferences about setting, characters, and events, and supports them with evidence from the text
- Interprets information from illustrations, diagrams, and graphic organizers
- Makes connections between texts and/or personal experiences
- Identifies and infers main idea and supporting details
- Self-monitors comprehension to clarify meaning
- Identifies the basic elements of a variety of genres (fiction, nonfiction, drama, and poetry)
- Recognizes the author's purpose
- Formulates and defends an opinion about a text

## Writing

The student demonstrates competency in the writing process.

- Captures a reader's interest by setting a purpose and developing a point of view
- Begins to select a focus and an organizational pattern based on purpose, genre, expectations, audience, and length
- Writes text of a length appropriate to address the topic or tell the story
- Uses organizational patterns for conveying information
- Begins to use specific sensory details to enhance descriptive effect
- Begins to develop characters through action and dialogue
- Begins to use descriptive adjectives and verbs to communicate setting, character, and plot
- Writes a response to literature that demonstrates understanding of the text, formulates an opinion, and supports a judgment
- Prewrites to generate ideas, develops a rough draft, rereads to revise, and edits to correct
- Publishes by presenting an edited piece of writing to others

## Listening, Speaking, and Viewing

The student uses oral and visual strategies to communicate.

- Adapts oral language to fit the situation by following the rules of conversation with peers and adults
- Uses oral language for different purposes: to inform, persuade, or entertain
- Listens to and views a variety of media to acquire information

We connect the core reading program and extended literacy curriculum to national and state standards to demonstrate the need for the extension of any core program. The extension of theme and reading practices allows readers time to investigate themes, genres, and text selections in depth. This time provides students with multiple opportunities to experience, and thus deepen their understanding of, the various standards in a wide variety of contexts.

## CHAPTER 5

# Getting Practical About Using the Best of Both: Questions and Answers

*When we take up literature in multiple ways, through who we are and how we think and communicate with others, we are engaging in literature. The words of the story lift off the page and enter into our social worlds. Rather than simply reading and comprehending text on a basic level, we are actively constructing meaning.*

— Shelby A. Wolf, *Interpreting Literature with Children*

Throughout this book we have shared possibilities for creating a literacy curriculum that combines the science of a core program with the art of teaching children's literature. Although we know that these aspects of teaching do not divide so easily, they do provide a beginning thinking point to this process of using both. The process of combining both requires careful thought and reflection. Literature and activities must be chosen with care so that they support a cohesive program of literacy instruction and learning for students. In this chapter, we take the reflective process that we engaged in as shared in chapters Two, Three, and Four, and make it explicit. We have organized this chapter around the questions that we hear from teachers as we share this process. We hope they stir your creativity and curiosity as you and your colleagues begin your explorations into both the science and art of teaching reading.

## "How" Questions

### Where do I find the time?

Until you carve a block of time from your daily schedule, it's probably not possible on a consistent basis to use both your core program and children's literature. If you find only a few moments in your weekly teaching schedule, using both a core program and children's literature will be ineffective. Finding consistent time is a planning activity that we think is best done with the principal, literacy coaches if they are a part of the school staff, and grade-level teachers. You will want to carefully consider all content expectations, any fixed limitations such as a literacy block requirement for the core program, and the set number of daily minutes required for content instruction. Once all the constraints on your time are placed on a daily schedule, uncommitted time can be devoted to two literacy blocks. In Chapter One, there are two sample schedules to consider that may help with this planning. In some cases, the second block may be limited to about a half hour, as this is all the time that can be squeezed into a tight teaching schedule. Even if this is the case, students benefit from this instruction for two and a half hours each week.

## After time is found for teaching both, what should happen next in planning?

This question has a twofold response. We always suggest that you carefully consider the language arts standards in your district and state first. We see these standards as fundamental to learning activities that are planned. You need to reassure your principal, your community of teachers, and the parents of your students that you are teaching to the language arts standards that have been adopted. You may also want to consider national language arts standards, as we have done in chapters Two, Three, and Four. Once you have a firm grasp of the language arts standards, you can discover children's books and activities that support student development.

The second part of this answer centers on the core reading program. We recommend that you consider each week of instruction under a theme, as most core reading programs are organized around themes. First, we suggest you review all of the text selections in the core anthology. After you are aware of all of the selections available (see Chapter Three for an example), you can select one for literature extension. The following are a few suggestions to help with the selection process.

The selection is of sufficient quality to return to for multiple exposures because:
- The text is well written.
- The illustrations are unique.
- The characters or plot are well developed and provide goal models.

The selection opens up other possibilities—for instance, other texts by the same author or illustrator or the exploration of a significant theme.

Because this is not a once-only process, feel free to choose other selections from the core anthology in successive years. For instance, if during the first year you zero in on one text and find that it does not sufficiently meet the learning needs of your students, during the next year you can make a different selection. In other situations, you may find that after using the same selection as the benchmark text over multiple years, you develop additional learning opportunities for students each year, thus having a wider repertoire to choose from to better meet the learning needs of your students.

## How should I work with the core reading program?

As we wrote earlier, many schools, and therefore teachers, are expected to use a core reading program for a 90-minute uninterrupted block of instruction. The goal for this focus is that children have a consistent curriculum that targets all major areas of literacy: phonemic awareness, phonics, comprehension, vocabulary, and fluency.

Authors of these programs always provide more instructional suggestions than teachers can ever use, so you may need to make important decisions about what you will teach and how. The process for these decisions might follow this sequence.

1. Explore the theme. Acquaint yourself with the theme resources (reading selections in the anthology, decodable books, leveled text, suggested library books, technology resources, and practice activities) and consider which will best meet the needs of your students. Many programs provide a few pages that share the theme at a glance. This overview helps you consider the materials and learning expectations of the theme.

2. Narrow the theme focus to the instruction that occurs during the block. For instance, many core reading programs offer a full range of language arts instruction. During the block, grammar may be excluded from writing instruction since there is a separate block devoted to grammar. It's best not to just tack on writing to reading instruction. So when children write during the block, it is most often first-draft writing whose purpose is sharing ideas to deepen comprehension or vocabulary knowledge.

3. Shift from the theme's organization to the first week of instruction. Decide how the anthology selection is used across the week. Investigate the recommended text for differentiated instruction and read it carefully so you are prepared to help students make connections across texts. Finally, consider the skills and strategies that are to be taught; you will likely give preference to targeted skills and strategies for direct instruction, as you know that these are the skills and strategies for which your students will be held accountable.

4. Carefully consider the lesson or instructional strategies suggested during the reading of the anthology selection. For instance, in the story *The Day Jimmy's Boa Ate the Wash*, one recommendation is that children predict what they might find out from a trip to a farm in preparation for reading. We think this prediction strategy could be enhanced by asking students to predict what they might see on a field trip to a farm and charting their predictions. After students read the book, have them share what they see in the book's illustrations that suggest what happened on this particular field trip. These two lists then serve as a comparison between a real and a fantasy trip to the farm.

After considering the prereading suggestions, you could evaluate the questions that the publisher offers. In some cases, you may decide to eliminate some of the suggested questions if they seem irrelevant to the text. For instance, in this story, the first question asks who is talking. We find this question unnecessary for most children as it is well supported in the illustrations. Most of the literal questions, if at all necessary, can be answered with whole-class responses. Other questions mix text and illustration comprehension. For instance, one question focuses on the mother's facial expression and another on how an egg broke on a child's head. The questions refer to the illustrations in some instances and the text in others, but this is never made explicit to students. If these questions are used, we would help students understand that in picture books the text and illustrations support each other, and students would decide if they answered the question through text, illustration support, or both. Moreover, since the major goal of this story is for children to understand cause-and-effect relationships, we would give preference to the questions that target these relationships.

To support this understanding, children can build a chart as you model the cause-and-effect happenings throughout this story (see Chapter Three). Further, we would give preference to questions that offer opportunities to discuss the text at more sophisticated levels, such as inferential and/or critical questions. For instance, children could respond to "Why would Jimmy bring a boa on the field trip?" or "Why did the adults let the children behave the way they did on this field trip?" While there are no right or wrong answers, students would use text and/or illustrations to support their responses. We suggest placing sticky notes in your edition with the revision of questions so that you remember these changes the next time you use this selection. See Chapter Four for additional suggestions for working with comprehension questions suggested by publishers.

5. Carefully scrutinize the leveled text that accompanies the core reading selection. The goal of using these books in small groups is to extend the learning that occurred during the sharing

of the anthology. Continue to practice new vocabulary words and the major comprehension strategy. The small-group setting allows you to engage in more personal conversations with your students about a text and the connections they make with it.

6. Carefully consider the activities that children are participating in as you work with small groups of students. We recommend that students engage primarily in reading and writing activities during this time. They might reread the anthology text or leveled text and write a response about the text they read. They might find interesting words during their reading and add them to their vocabulary notebooks. They might record interesting facts from the text selection. All these activities support reading and writing for independent practice. You can easily monitor the amount of time that students are reading and/or writing during independent time by conducting a quick scan of the class. If most students are filling in blanks on a worksheet or coloring, their time is not being used to enhance their reading and writing knowledge and skill.

## How should I plan for the literature block?

We recommend that you decide how you will use literature to narrow your focus in selecting children's literature and activities. For instance, you may choose an author or illustrator study or a content-focused extension. Once the focus is decided, the next step is to find children's literature. Following are several ways to accomplish this task.

1. Check with the school and community librarians. They can share the books they have available for checkout. We have found that community libraries will often lend up to 40 books at a time for teacher use.

2. Check your personal classroom library. If your library is limited, it is time to enrich it. There are easy ways to do this. One way is to use Scholastic Book Club in your classroom. When children purchase books, teachers have the opportunity to order free books. Additionally, you may want to purchase books from children's book catalogues. Another way is to visit garage sales, where people often sell children's books for very low cost. Deciding on which books to purchase is easier through the targeting of certain areas for extended literature exploration, although in our case we always find books that we didn't plan to buy because we are sure they will be engaging to students. Be warned—buying children's books can and will become an addiction.

3.  Chat with teachers at your school who may have books to fit your topic or theme and are willing to lend them.

4.  Visit local bookstores to peruse children's books and perhaps purchase some.

5.  Visit Web sites. Here are some that we've found helpful.
    *   **www.carolhurst.com** This site provides a newsletter about children's books. There are also children's books organized by theme and curricular area.
    *   **www.ucalgary.ca/~dkbrown** This site provides information about children's books, authors, and award winners. There are resources for teachers that include teaching ideas linked to children's books. It also provides numerous links to authors' and illustrators' Web sites.
    *   **www.icdlbooks.org** This site offers books from around the world. In many cases the books can be accessed from this site. When we visited this site, we read the book *Estrellita*, a book written by a Filipino author.
    *   **www.ala.org** This site provides links to a great variety of Web sites devoted to children's literature. There are also articles about children's literature available to teachers.
    *   **reading.indiana.edu** This site is the clearinghouse for reading, English, and communication. There are several databases that focus on children's literature.
    *   **www.lib.muohio.edu/pictbks** This site allows teachers to search children's books by topics or concepts.
    *   **www.readwritethink.org** This site is sponsored by the National Council of Teachers of English and the International Reading Association. Teachers provide lessons for a variety of children's books. Each lesson has a research article to support the strategy being used, full details for the lesson, and Web resources.
    *   **www.scholastic.com** and **www.scholastic.com/kids** These sites offer lists of books to select and activities to use with students.

6.  Visit the Web sites of the core program in use. These sites often share related children's literature and activities. The Web site locations are always listed in the teacher's edition.

7.  Read journals centered on children's literature.
    *   *The Reading Teacher.* This journal is published by the International Reading Association and features a section devoted to children's literature. (www.reading.org)
    *   *Language Arts.* This journal is published by the National Council of Teachers of English. It has a section in each issue devoted to children's literature. (www.ncte.org)

- *Book Links.* This journal is focused on children's literature. (P.O. Box 1347, Elmhurst, IL 60126)
- *The Horn Book.* This journal is focused on children's literature. (Park Square Building, 31 Saint James Avenue, Boston, MA 02116)
- *CBC Features.* This journal is focused on children's literature. (Children's Book Council, Inc. 350 Scotland Rd., Orange, NJ 07050)

8. Choose activities connected to children's literature that best support the literacy learning of students. This brainstorming of possible activities is best done with grade-level teachers. Here teachers take each part of their language arts curriculum and plan activities. (Later in the chapter we offer many suggestions.) We suggested a template in previous chapters to guide the choice of activities. We brainstormed around the following areas:
   a. Reading Connections (Fiction and Nonfiction)
   b. Writing Connections
   c. Author or Illustrator Studies
   d. Extension of Core Theme
   e. Vocabulary Extensions
   f. Fluency
   g. Visual Literacy Extensions
   h. Connections to Technology

Once a wealth of activities are developed, you can select those that are most appropriate for your students and best target their learning goals.

# "What" Questions

These questions center on the possibilities for reading and writing activities central to comprehension. Reading and writing activities offer children authentic ways to participate as readers and writers as they develop knowledge and skill. The activities that are documented are still just a small subset of what teachers may envision for students. We also maintain that it is not necessary to change activities on a daily basis. Students do not get bored writing about their reading each day, for instance. Our goal here is to suggest possibilities, not to create a list that must be worked through systematically, so that all effective practices have a chance to shine in the classroom.

- **Retelling a story.** Children retell a story to a peer or they write a retelling of the text they read.

- **Sequencing story events.** Children do a quick sketch and write about what happened at the beginning, middle, and end of a story. To facilitate this process with young children, fold the paper into thirds. As children gain skill with sequencing story events, they can be expected to retell more of the events within a story.

- **Sequencing main events in a story with a stair-step format.** Students are provided an organizer that facilitates recording of major events (see Figure 5.1).

- **Description of a character or setting.** The student does a quick sketch of a character or the setting and then provides words or sentences to describe either.

- **Retelling of an informational concept with a graphic organizer.** The student uses a graphic organizer to describe a topic or share a sequence, such as the life of a butterfly, or provides cause-and-effect details in an appropriate organizer. It is important to this strategy that the graphic organizer match the task. A cluster would be appropriate for description, a timeline for a time-related sequence, a T-chart or Venn diagram for comparison, and an arrow chart for cause-and-effect relationships.

- **Written response.** Students write about their reading. They can share their responses with fellow students or with the teachers and a small group of students. Students can use a response notebook—a spiral-bound notebook—so that responses are not lost.

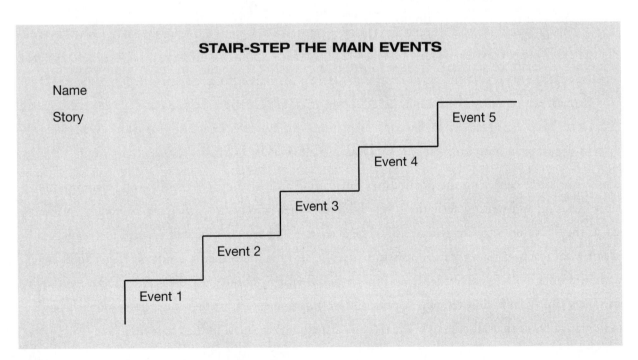

FIGURE 5.1: Stair-step format for sequencing main events

- **Sketch to stretch.** The process begins with students reading a portion of text (Harste, Short, & Burke, 1989). When students complete their reading, they write a response in their notebook. You could then guide a discussion about the theme of the narrative. Students then do a quick sketch of the theme. Students share and discuss their sketches, and they can revise them following discussion.

- **Dialogical-thinking reading lesson.** This strategy was designed by Commeyras (1990) to teach critical-thinking skills. Students are asked to respond to questions that have multiple interpretations. A model question for "Jack and the Beanstalk" might be "Why would the giant's wife help Jack?" Students can discuss these questions in small groups and then write their own personal response.

- **Data charts.** Students record information that they find about a topic in a table or chart. Each column lists an aspect of what they are studying, such as where an animal lives, its predators, and so on. When the student finds information about an aspect of his or her topic, it is recorded with its citation in the block under the heading. As this chart is completed, students have a record of the information they have located, which supports their writing about the topic.

- **Learning logs.** Students record information in a learning log that they can refer to for further reading or writing. For example, they may list the parts of a frog or the frog's life cycle.

- **"I wonder" bookmarks.** Students have a bookmark with several "I wonder" statements and spaces to write what they wonder and to record a page number (see Figure 5.2) (McLaughlin & Fisher, 2005). These bookmarks can be used for discussion among students or with a small group of students and their teacher.

- **Summarizing.** Students write a summary of an important idea shared in their reading.

- **Evaluating.** Students make judgments about the book they are reading. They support these evaluations with samples of text.

Name _____

Page _____

I wonder

FIGURE 5.2: "I wonder" bookmark

- **Question-answer relationships.** As students answer questions, they decide whether the answer was right on the page (Right There) or whether they have to use more than one piece of text to answer the question (Think and Search) (Raphael, 1986). There are also questions that require more than the text to answer, such as those that require both text and personal knowledge (Author and Me), or questions that rely solely on the reader (On My Own). As a student answers a question, he or she records the type of question it is.

- **Double-entry journal.** Students copy portions of text and then

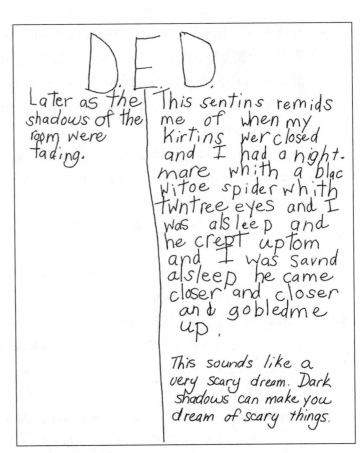

FIGURE 5.3: Double-entry draft response

record the reasons they chose this particular text snippet (Barone, 1990). Figure 5.3 shares an example of a double-entry draft response. On the left is the part copied from a text, on the right is the student's response, and at the bottom is the teacher's comment.

# "Why" Questions

We have addressed most of the "why" questions throughout this book. We argue that neither a core reading program nor a literature-based curriculum are sufficient on their own for literacy instruction for young children. We consider both to be necessary in providing a complete literacy program that supports the skills and strategies of reading and writing as well as the joy and motivation for reading and writing.

We have collected numerous quotations from others to support this view. We present them here as encouragement as you begin the process of using and benefiting from the science and art of helping your students become passionate, skillful, successful readers.

*Simply being able to decode and answer low-level literal questions about a piece of text is no longer sufficient. Becoming fully literate has come to mean, among other things, using strategies independently to construct meaning from text, using text information to build conceptual understanding, effectively communicating ideas orally and in writing, and developing the intrinsic desire to read and write.*

(Gambrell, Malloy, & Mazzoni, 2007, p. 13)

*Throughout the years, four major approaches—phonics, basal, literature, and language experience/writing—have been in and out of favor. Generally, one approach has predominated just long enough for people to recognize its shortcomings and is then abandoned in favor of a different approach with different shortcomings. Asking which method is best cannot be answered, because it is the wrong question. Each method has undeniable strengths.*

(Hall, Prevatte, & Cunningham, 1995, p. 139)

*Reducing the curriculum to low-level skills that require little thinking with text minimizes the chance that the students will gain ownership and control of what they learn so that they can apply it to new situations. Students should spend most of their time actually reading rather than on useless seatwork or other activities that do not directly support learning to read.*

(Strickland, 2002, p. 79)

*Whether we are discussing literature, investigating the relationship between written symbols and oral language, helping readers choose an appropriate book to read independently, or working on understanding the nature of the alphabet, I am constantly assessing how the practices and procedures I am enacting in my reading workshop serve the primary goal of supporting readers' construction of meaning in transactions with text.*

(Serafini, 2006, p. 2)

*In my own work and that of my closest colleagues, the classrooms where reading and writing seem to be developing best are ones in which there is a lot of coverage of skills and a great deal of teacher support as children apply the skills they are learning to the reading of excellent literature and to writing.*

(Pressley, 2006b, p. 427)

*Direct instruction in decoding and comprehension skills is balanced with opportunities to listen to interesting stories and to engage in enjoyable, self-selected reading and writing activities.*

(Christie, Enz, & Vukelich, 2003, p. 199)

*Effective teachers of reading use literature, whether published as trade books or contained in commercial reading programs, to teach reading. Literature is the core of a balanced literacy program because of its universal appeal. As they read, students meet characters they can relate to and heroes who grapple with all of life's tragedies, joys, and triumphs. Students learn about the world around them and are vicariously transported to other lands or back or forward in time to experience lives very different from their own.*
(Tompkins, 2001, p. 28)

*For all students, including young children, struggling learners, and second-language learners, access to books and time spent reading leads to growth in vocabulary, knowledge, language and literacy skills, general intelligence, and achievement.*
(Worthy & Roser, 2004, p. 180)

*It is essential that children have many opportunities to read and write, especially school-day opportunities to read comfortable materials they have chosen and to discuss them with peers. To accomplish this requires greater access to a wider variety of appropriate reading material beyond the basal reader, the core trade book, or the common social studies textbook. It also requires substantial time be available every day in every classroom to engage in reading and writing activities.*
(Allington & Cunningham, 2002, p. 65)

We revisit these quotes when the transition to using both seems difficult. They support us over the changes in curriculum that require thinking and rethinking as they become routines. They sustain us on difficult days when our plans seem not to work. They encourage us when students find the expected thinking about reading and writing difficult to attain. They inspire us to continue as we recognize the importance of using both to develop readers and writers.

## Beyond Questions

Now it is time to get started. Invite, encourage, or cajole your grade-level colleagues as needed to join with you as you explore using both your core reading program and quality children's literature. Work together on your first exploration so that you can share ideas and planning. Find time to chat and reflect on how it is going. Consider student writing and what it shows about comprehension. Ask students what they are learning and thinking about through these explorations. Ask them about the books they are reading. Enjoy what you discover. Smile! Now you are an exemplary teacher who can use both the science and the art of teaching.

# $\mathcal{P}$rofessional References Cited

Allington, R., & Cunningham, P. (2002). *Schools that work.* Boston: Allyn & Bacon.

Anderson, N. (2006). *Elementary children's literature: The basics for teachers and parents* (2nd ed.). Boston: Allyn & Bacon.

Anstey, M., & Bull, G. (2006). *Teaching and learning multiliteracies: Changing times, changing literacies.* Newark, DE: International Reading Association.

Barone, D. (1990). The written responses of young children: Beyond comprehension to story understanding. *The New Advocate, 3,* 49–56.

Barone, D., & Taylor, J. (2007). *The practical guide to classroom literacy assessment.* Thousand Oaks, CA: Corwin Press.

Barone, D., Mallette, M., & Xu, S. (2005). *Teaching early literacy: Development, assessment, and instruction.* New York: Guilford Press.

Bean, R. (2002). Developing an effective reading program. In S. Wepner, D. Strickland, & J. Feeley (Eds.), *The administration and supervision of reading programs* (3rd ed., pp. 3–15). New York: Teachers College Press.

Christie, J., Enz, B., & Vukelich, C. (2003). *Teaching language and literacy.* Boston: Allyn & Bacon.

Cochran-Smith, M. (1984). *The making of a reader.* Norwood, NJ: Ablex.

Commeyras, M. (1990). Analyzing a critical-thinking reading lesson. *Teaching and Teacher Education, 6,* 210–214.

Culham, R. (2005). *6 + 1 traits of writing: The complete guide for the primary grades.* New York: Scholastic.

Dahl, K., & Freppon, P. (1995). A comparison of inner-city children's interpretations of reading and writing instruction in the early grades in skills-based and whole language classrooms. *Reading Research Quarterly, 30,* 50–74.

Elley, W. (1989). Vocabulary acquisition from listening to stories. *Reading Research Quarterly, 24,* 174–187.

Fawson, P., & Reutzel, R. (2000). But I only have a basal: Implementing guided reading in the early grades. *The Reading Teacher, 54*, 84–97.

Foresman, S. (2004). *Take a closer look.* (Scott Foresman core reading program.) Upper Saddle River, NJ: Pearson Scott Foresman.

Gambrell, L., & Mazzoni, S. (1999). Principles of best practice: Finding the common ground. In L. Gambrell, L. Morrow, S. Neuman, & M. Pressley (Eds.), *Best practices in literacy instruction* (pp. 11–21). New York: Guilford Press.

Gambrell, L., Malloy, J., & Mazzoni, S. (2007). Evidence-based best practices for comprehensive literacy instruction. In L. Gambrell, L. Morrow, & M. Pressley (Eds.), *Best practices in literacy instruction* (pp. 11-29). New York: Guilford Press.

Good, R., Simmons, D., & Kame'enui, E. (2002). The importance and decision-making utility of a continuum of fluency-based indicators of foundational reading skills for third-grade high-stakes outcomes. In U.S. Department of Education (Ed.), *The reading leadership academy guidebook* (pp. 1–29). Washington, DC: U.S. Department of Education.

Goodman, K. (1986). *What's whole in whole language?* Richmond Hill, Ontario, Canada: Scholastic.

Hall, D., Prevatte, C., & Cunningham, P. (1995). Eliminating ability grouping and reducing failure in the primary grades. In R. Allington & S. Walmsley (Eds.), *No quick fix* (pp. 137–158). New York: Teachers College Press.

Harste, J., Short, K., & Burke, C. (1989). *Creating classrooms for authors: The reading/writing connection.* Portsmouth, NH: Heinemann.

Hoffman, J., McCarthey, S., Elliot, B., Bayles, D., Price, D., Ferree, A., & Abbott, J. (1998). The literature-based basals in first-grade classrooms: Savior, Satan, or same-old, same-old? *Reading Research Quarterly, 33*, 168–197.

Houghton Mifflin (2005). *Houghton Mifflin reading: Theme three, incredible stories.* Boston: Houghton Mifflin.

Hudak-Huelbig, E., Keyes, M., McClure, A., & Stellingwerf, E. (1991). *You can't judge a basal by its cover: A comparison of seven basal reader series.* Unpublished report, William Paterson College, Wayne, NJ.

Kucan, L., Lapp, D., Flood, J., & Fisher, D. (2007). Institutional resources in the classroom: Deepening understanding through interaction with multiple texts and multiple media. In L. Gambrell & M. Pressley (Eds.), *Best Practices in Literacy Instruction* (pp. 285–312). New York: Guilford Press.

Lapp, D., Fisher, D., Flood, J., Goss-Moore, K., & Moore, J. (2002). Selecting materials for the literacy program. In S. Wepner, D. Strickland, & J. Feeley (Eds.), *The administration and supervision of reading programs* (3rd ed., pp. 83–94). New York: Teachers College Press.

McLaughlin, M., & Fisher, L. (2005). *Research-based reading lessons for K–3*. New York: Scholastic.

Mitchell, D. (2003). *Children's literature*. Boston: Allyn and Bacon.

Morrow, L. (1991). Relationships among physical designs of play centers, teachers' emphasis on literacy in play, and children's literacy behaviors during play. In J. Zutell & S. McCormick (Eds.), *Learner factors/teacher factors: Issues in literacy research and instruction—fortieth yearbook of the National Reading Conference* (pp. 127–140). Chicago: National Reading Conference.

National Reading Panel. (2000). *Teaching children to read: An evidence-based assessment of the scientific research literature on reading and its implications for reading instruction: Reports of the subgroups.* Washington, DC: National Institute of Child Health and Development.

Nystrand, M. (1997). *Opening dialogue: Understanding the dynamics of language and learning in the English classroom*. New York: Teachers College Press.

Peterson, R., & Eeds, M. (2007). *Grand conversations: Literature groups in action*. New York: Scholastic.

Popp, H. (1975). Current practices in the teaching of beginning reading. In J. Carroll & J. Chall (Eds.), *Toward a literate society* (pp. 101–146). New York: McGraw-Hill.

Pressley, M. (2006a). Concluding reflections. In M. Pressley (Ed.), *Reading instruction that works* (pp. 417–448). New York: Guilford Press.

Pressley, M. (2006b). *Reading instruction that works: A case for balanced teaching*. New York: Guilford Press.

Pressley, M., Allington, R., Wharton-McDonald, R., Block, C., & Morrrow, L. (2001). *Learning to read: Lessons from exemplary first-grade classrooms*. New York: Guilford Press.

Pressley, M., Rankin, J., & Yokoi, L. (1996). A survey of instructional practices of primary grade teachers nominated as effective in promoting literacy. *Elementary School Journal, 96*, 363–384.

Raphael, T. (1986). Teaching children question-answer relationships, revisited. *The Reading Teacher, 39*, 516–522.

Serafini, F., & Giorgis, C. (2003). *Reading aloud and beyond: Fostering intellectual life with older readers*. Portsmouth, NH: Heinemann.

Serafini, F., & Youngs, S. (2008). *More (advanced) lessons in comprehension: Expanding students' understanding of all types of texts.* Portsmouth, NH: Heinemann.

Serafini, F. (2004). *Lessons in comprehension: Explicit instruction in the reading workshop.* Portsmouth, NH: Heinemann.

Serafini, F. (2006). *Around the reading workshop in 180 days.* Portsmouth, NH: Heinemann.

Sipe, L. (1993a). Using transformations of traditional stories: Making the reading-writing connection. *The Reading Teacher, 47,* 18–26.

Smith, F. (1979). *Reading without nonsense.* New York: Teachers College Press.

Snow, C., Burns, M., & Griffin, P. (1998). *Preventing reading difficulties in young children.* Washington, DC: National Academy Press.

Strickland, D. (2002). The importance of effective early intervention. In A. Farstrup & J. Samuels (Eds.), *What research has to say about reading instruction* (pp. 69–86). Newark, DE: International Reading Association.

Taylor, B., & Pearson, P. (2002). *Teaching reading: Effective schools, accomplished teachers.* Mahwah, NH: Lawrence Erlbaum Associates.

Taylor, B., Pearson, P. D., Clark, K., & Walpole, S. (1999). Effective schools/accomplished teachers. *The Reading Teacher, 53,* 156–159.

Tompkins, G. (2001). *Literacy for the 21st century.* Upper Saddle River, NJ: Merrill Prentice Hall.

Weaver, C. (2002). *Reading process and practice* (3rd ed.) Portsmouth, NH: Heinemann.

Wepner, S., Strickland, D., & Feeley, J. (Eds.). (2002). *The administration and supervision of reading programs* (3rd ed.). New York: Teachers College Press.

Wolf, S. (2004). *Interpreting literature with children.* Mahwah, NJ: Lawrence Erlbaum Associates.

Worthy, J., & Roser, N. (2004). Flood ensurance: When children have books they can and want to read. In D. Lapp, C. Block, E. Cooper, J. Flood, N. Roser, & J. Tinajero (Eds.), *Teaching all the children* (pp. 179–192). New York: Guilford Press.

# Children's Literature Cited

Adoff, A. (1988). *Greens.* New York: Lothrop, Lee & Shepard Books.

Ahlberg, J., & Ahlberg, A. (1986). *The Jolly Postman or Other People's Letters.* London: Heinemann.

Applegate, K. A. (1996). *The Encounter* (Animorphs #3). New York: Scholastic.

Arnosky, J. (2002). *All About Frogs.* New York: Scholastic.

Arnosky, J. (2002). *All About Rattlesnakes.* New York: Scholastic.

Babbit, N. (1985). *Tuck Everlasting.* New York: Farrar, Straus and Giroux.

Bakken, A. (2006). *Uncover a Frog.* San Diego: Silver Dolphin Books.

Barrett, J. (1978). *Cloudy With a Chance of Meatballs.* New York: Atheneum.

Base, G. (1996). *The Discovery of Dragons.* New York: Viking.

Bayer, J. (1987). *A, My Name is Alice.* New York: Puffin Books.

Bentley, D. (2000). *The Icky Sticky Frog.* Los Angeles: Piggy Toes Press.

Berger, M., & Berger, G. (2002). *How Do Frogs Swallow With Their Eyes?* New York: Scholastic.

Breen, S. (2007). *Stick.* New York: Dial Books.

Brooks, A. (1996). *Frogs Jump! A Counting Book.* New York: Scholastic.

Browne, A. (1990). *Changes.* London: Julia MacRae.

Browne, A. (1991). *Willy's Pictures.* Cambridge, MA: Candlewick Press.

Browne, A. (1992). *Zoo.* New York: Knopf.

Browne, A. (2001). *Voices in the Park.* New York: DK Publishing.

Burnford, S. (1961). *The Incredible Journey.* London: Hodder & Stoughton.

Burningham, J. (1977). *Come Away From the Water, Shirley.* New York: Crowell.

Butterfield, M., & Ford, W. (1998). *What Am I?* Austin, TX: Steck-Vaughn Company.

Cannon, J. (1997). *Stellaluna.* San Diego: Harcourt.

Cannon, J. (1997). *Verdi*. San Diego: Harcourt.

Carle, E. (1986). *Papa, Please Get the Moon for Me*. New York: Picture Book Studio.

Carle, E. (1994). *The Very Hungry Caterpillar*. New York: Philomel Company.

Conrad, P. (1990). *Stonewords*. New York: HarperCollins.

Coville, B. (1994). *Into the Land of the Unicorns*. New York: Scholastic.

Cowley, J. (2006). *Red-Eyed Tree Frog*. New York: Scholastic.

Cronin, D. (2000). *Click, Clack, Moo: Cows That Type*. New York: Simon & Schuster.

Dahl, R. (1982). *The BFG*. New York: Farrar, Straus and Giroux.

Dahl, R. (1988). *Matilda*. New York: Viking.

dePaola, T. (1984). *The Mysterious Giant of Barletta*. New York: Harcourt Brace Jovanovich.

DiCamillo, K. (2003). *The Tale of Despereaux: Being the Story of a Mouse, a Princess, Some Soup, and a Spool of Thread*. Cambridge, MA: Candlewick Press.

DK Publishing. (1997). *The Snake Book*. New York: DK Publishing.

Driscoll, L. (1998). *Frogs*. New York: Grosset & Dunlap.

Editors of *Time for Kids*. (2006). *Frogs!* New York: HarperCollins.

Erlich, A. (1998). *Leo, Zack, and Emmie Together Again*. New York: Puffin Books.

Falconer, I. (2001). *Olivia*. New York: Atheneum.

Fleischmann, S. (1986). *The Whipping Boy*. New York: Greenwillow Books.

Foley, C. (2000). *Find the Snake*. New York: Children's Press.

Fowler, A. (1992). *Frogs and Toads and Tadpoles, Too*. Chicago: Children's Press.

Fox, M. (1989). *Night Noises*. New York: Doubleday Dell Publishing Group, Inc.

French, F. (1990). *Snow White in New York*. New York: Oxford Publishing Services.

George, J. C. (1997). *Julie's Wolf Pack*. New York: HarperTrophy.

Gormley, B. (1996). *Back to the Day Lincoln Was Shot*. New York: Scholastic.

Gravett, E. (2006). *Wolves*. New York: Simon & Schuster.

Grimm, J., & Grimm, W. (2004). *The Annotated Brothers Grimm* (translator, Maria Tatar). New York: W. W. Norton & Company, Inc.

Guarino, D. (2002). *Is Your Mama a Llama?* New York: Scholastic.

Henkes, K. (1991). *Chrysanthemum.* New York: Greenwillow Books.

Henkes, K. (1996). *Lilly's Purple Plastic Purse.* New York: Greenwillow Books.

Henkes, K. (2004). *Kitten's First Full Moon.* New York: Greenwillow Books.

Hill, E. (2004). *Spot's First Walk.* New York: Puffin Books.

Howe, D., & Howe, J. (1996). *Bunnicula: A Rabbit-Tale of Mystery.* New York: Aladdin.

Irving, W. (1990). *Legend of Sleepy Hollow.* New York: William Morrow & Company, Inc.

James, S. (1996). *Dear Mr. Blueberry.* New York: Aladdin.

Jenkins, M. (2003). *The Emperor's Egg.* Cambridge, MA: Candlewick.

Jonas, A. (1983). *Round Trip.* New York: Scholastic.

Juster, N. (1989). *The Phantom Tollbooth.* New York: Yearling.

Juster, N. (2006). *The Hello Goodbye Window.* New York: Hyperion.

Kalan, R. (1981). *Jump, Frog, Jump.* New York: William Morrow & Company, Inc.

Kellogg, S. (1985). *Paul Bunyan.* New York: HarperTrophy.

Kellogg, S. (1986). *Pecos Bill.* New York: Scholastic.

Kellogg, S. (1988). *Johnny Appleseed.* New York: HarperCollins.

Kellogg, S. (1989). *Chicken Little.* Boston: Houghton Mifflin.

Kellogg, S. (1991). *Jack and the Beanstalk.* New York: William Morrow & Company, Inc.

Kellogg, S. (1992). *Best Friends.* New York: Puffin Books.

Kellogg, S. (1992). *Can I Keep Him?* New York: Puffin Books.

Kellogg, S. (1992). *The Christmas Witch.* New York: Dial Books.

Kellogg, S. (1993). *The Island of the Skog.* New York: Puffin Books.

Kellogg, S. (1996). *I Was Born About 10,000 Years Ago.* New York: William Morrow & Company, Inc.

Kellogg, S. (1996). *Yankee Doodle.* New York: Simon & Schuster.

Kellogg, S. (1997). *The Three Little Pigs.* New York: William Morrow & Company, Inc..

Kellogg, S. (1998). *Mike Fink.* New York: HarperTrophy.

Kellogg, S. (1999). *Sally Ann Thunder Ann Whirlwind Crockett: A Tall Tale*. New York: HarperTrophy.

Kellogg, S. (1999). *The Three Sillies*. Cambridge, MA: Candlewick Press.

Kellogg, S. (2000). *Give the Dog a Bone*. New York: SeaSTAR Books.

Kellogg, S. (2000). *The Missing Mitten Mystery*. New York: Dial Books.

Kellogg, S. (2001). *A Penguin Pup for Pinkerton*. New York: Dial Books.

Kellogg, S. (2001). *A-Hunting We Will Go!* New York: HarperTrophy.

Kellogg, S. (2002). *A Rose for Pinkerton*. New York: Puffin Books.

Kellogg, S. (2002). *Pinkerton, Behave*. New York: Dial Books.

Kellogg, S. (2002). *Prehistoric, Pinkerton*. New York: Puffin Books.

Kellogg, S. (2002). *Tallyho, Pinkerton*. New York: Dial Books.

Kellogg, S. (2002). *The Mysterious Tadpole*. New York: Dial Books.

Kellogg, S. (2004). *Pinkerton and Friends*. New York: Dial Books.

Kinerk, R. (2007). *Clorinda Takes Flight*. New York: Simon & Schuster.

Kotzwinkle, W., & Murray, G. (2001). *Walter the Farting Dog*. Berkeley, CA: North Atlantic.

Le Guin, U. K. (1989). *Catwing's Return*. New York: Orchard Books.

Lehman, B. (2005). *The Red Book*. Boston: Houghton Mifflin.

Lester, J. (1994). *John Henry*. New York: Dial Books.

Lewis, J. (1994). *The Frog Princess*. New York: Dial Books.

Lionni, L. (1967). *Frederick*. New York: Pantheon.

Lobel, A. (1979). *Days with Frog and Toad*. New York: Scholastic.

Lobel. A. (1979). *Frog and Toad Are Friends*. New York: HarperCollins.

London, J. (1996). *Froggy Goes to School*. New York: Puffin Books.

London, J. (2003). *The Call of the Wild*. New York: Aladdin.

Macaulay, D. (1987). *Why the Chicken Crossed the Road*. Boston: Houghton Mifflin.

Macaulay, D. (1990). *Black and White*. Boston: Houghton Mifflin.

Macaulay, D. (1995). *Shortcut.* Boston: Houghton Mifflin.

MacLulich, C. (1996). *Frogs.* New York: Scholastic.

Mahy, M. (1993). *The Boy Who Was Followed Home.* New York: Dial Books.

Mahy, M. (1994). *Rattlebang Picnic.* New York: Dial Books.

Martin, B. (2000). *A Beastly Story.* New York: Scholastic.

Martin, R. (1989). *Will's Mammoth.* New York: Doubleday Dell Publishing Group, Inc.

Massie, D. (2000). *The Baby Beebee Bird.* New York: HarperCollins.

Mayer, M. (1968). *There's a Nightmare in My Closet.* New York: Dial Books.

Milne, A. A. (1926). *Winnie-the-Pooh.* New York: Dell.

Noble, T. (1992). *Jimmy's Boa Bounces Back.* New York: Puffin Books.

Noble, T. (1992). *The Day Jimmy's Boa Ate the Wash.* New York: Puffin Books.

Noble, T. (1993). *Jimmy's Boa and the Big Splash Birthday Bash.* New York: Puffin Books.

Noble, T. (2005). *Jimmy's Boa and the Bungee Jump Slam Dunk.* New York: Puffin Books.

Nolen, P. (1998). *Raising Dragons.* New York: Silver Whistle Publishers.

Ormerod, J. (1990). *The Frog Prince.* New York: William Morrow & Company, Inc.

Pallotta, J. (2006). *Snakes: Long, Longer, Longest.* New York: Scholastic.

Paradise, M. (1998). *Imaginary Insects.* Topeka, KS: Studentreasures Publishing Co.

Parenteau, S. (2007). *One Frog Sang.* New York: Candlewick Press.

Parker, V. (2004). *Life as a Frog.* Chicago: Raintree.

Patent, D. (2003). *Slinky Scaly Slithery Snakes.* New York: Scholastic.

Patent, D. (1997). *Flashy Fantastic Rain Forest Frogs.* New York: Scholastic.

Paxton, T. (1995). *Engelbert the Elephant.* New York: William Morrow & Company, Inc.

Pilkey, D. (1993). *Dogzilla.* San Diego: Harcourt.

Potter, B. (1999). *The Tale of Peter Rabbit.* London: Penguin.

Poydar, N. (1996). *Cool Ali.* New York: Margaret K. McElderry.

Prelutsky, J. (1983). *The Random House Book of Poetry for Children.* New York: Random House.

Preston-Mafham, K. (1999). *Frogs and Toads.* London: Quintet Publishing Ltd.

Riches, S. (2000). *Fat Frogs on a Skinny Log.* New York: Scholastic.

Ringgold, F. (1992). *Tar Beach.* New York: Random House.

Robb, L. (1995). *Snuffles and Snouts.* New York: Dial Books.

Robinson, F. (1993). *A Frog Inside My Hat.* New York: Troll Medallion.

Robinson, F. (1996). *Great Snakes.* New York: Scholastic.

Robinson, F. (1999). *Amazing Lizards!* New York: Scholastic.

Robinson, F. (1999). *Fantastic Frogs!* New York: Scholastic.

Rohmann, E. (2002). *My Friend Rabbit.* Brookfield, CT: Roaring Brook Press.

Rosenberg, L. (1993). *Monster Mama.* New York: Doubleday Dell Publishing Group, Inc.

Ryder, J. (2002). *Big Bear Ball.* New York: HarperCollins.

Rylant, C. (2006). *The Van Gogh Café.* New York: Harcourt.

Rylant, C. (1996). *Henry and Mudge and the Happy Cat.* New York: Aladdin.

Rylant, C. (1999). *The Islander.* New York: Random House.

Sachar, L. (1998). *Sideways Stories from Wayside School.* New York: Knopf.

Say, A. (2002). *Home of the Brave.* New York: Houghton Mifflin.

Say, A. (1995). *Stranger in the Mirror.* New York: Houghton Mifflin.

Schwartz, A. (1981). *Scary Stories to Tell in the Dark.* Hagerstown, MD: Lippincott.

Schwartz, D. (1985). *How Much Is a Million?* New York: Scholastic.

Schwartz, D. (1989). *If You Made a Million.* New York: Lothrop, Lee & Shepard Books.

Schwartz, D. (1999). *If You Hopped Like a Frog.* New York: Scholastic.

Schwartz, D. (2003). *Millions to Measure.* New York: HarperCollins.

Scieszka, J. Time Warp Trio series. New York: Viking.

Scieszka, J. (1992). *The Stinky Cheese Man and Other Fairly Stupid Tales.* New York: Viking.

Scieszka, J. (1991). *The Frog Prince Continued.* New York: Puffin Books.

Selden, G. (1991). *The Cricket in Times Square.* New York: Farrar, Straus and Giroux.

Sendak, M. (1991). *Where the Wild Things Are*. New York: HarperCollins.

Sharmat, M. (1987). *Gila Monsters Meet You at the Airport*. New York: Puffin Books.

Simon, S. (1994). *Snakes*. New York: HarperTrophy.

Sis, P. (1996). *Starry Messenger*. New York: Frances Foster.

Steig, W. (1969). *Sylvester and the Magic Pebble*. New York: Aladdin Paperbacks.

Steig, W. (1984). *Dominic*. New York: Farrar, Straus and Giroux.

Stewart, D. (1998). *From Tadpole to Frog*. New York: Scholastic.

Tarcov, E. (1974). *The Frog Prince*. New York: Scholastic.

Teague, M. (1997). *How I Spent My Summer Vacation*. New York: Dragonfly Books.

Teague, M. (2002). *Dear Mrs. LaRue: Letters from Obedience School*. New York: Scholastic.

Thompson, C. (1993). *Looking for Atlantis*. New York: Knopf.

Thurber, J. (1994). *The Great Quillow*. New York: Harcourt.

Van Allsburg, C. (1979). *The Garden of Abdul Gasazi*. Boston: Houghton Mifflin.

Van Allsburg, C. (1981). *Jumanji*. Boston: Houghton Mifflin.

Van Allsburg, C. (1982). *Ben's Dream*. Boston: Houghton Mifflin.

Van Allsburg, C. (1983). *The Wreck of the Zephyr*. Boston: Houghton Mifflin.

Van Allsburg, C. (1984). *The Mysteries of Harris Burdick*. Boston: Houghton Mifflin.

Van Allsburg, C. (1985). *The Polar Express*. New York: Houghton Mifflin.

Van Allsburg, C. (1986). *The Stranger*. Boston: Houghton Mifflin.

Van Allsburg, C. (1987). *The Z Was Zapped*. Boston: Houghton Mifflin.

Van Allsburg, C. (1988). *Two Bad Ants*. Boston: Houghton Mifflin.

Van Allsburg, C. (1990). *Just a Dream*. Boston: Houghton Mifflin.

Van Allsburg, C. (1991). *The Wretched Stone*. Boston: Houghton Mifflin.

Van Allsburg, C. (1992). *The Widow's Broom*. Boston: Houghton Mifflin.

Van Allsburg, C. (1993). *The Sweetest Fig*. Boston: Houghton Mifflin.

Van Allsburg, C. (1995). *Bad Day at Riverbend*. Boston: Houghton Mifflin.

Van Allsburg, C. (2002). *Zathura: A Space Adventure*. New York: Houghton Mifflin.

Van Allsburg, C. (2006). *Probuditi!* New York: Houghton Mifflin.

Viorst, J. (1994). *The Alphabet from Z to A*. New York: Atheneum.

Wang, M. (1986). *The Frog Prince*. Chicago: Children's Press.

White, E. B. (1952). *Charlotte's Web*. New York: HarperCollins.

Wiesner, D. (1991). *Tuesday*. New York: Clarion.

Wiesner, D. (2001). *The Three Pigs*. New York: Clarion.

Wiesner, D. (2007). *Flotsam*. New York: Clarion.

Willard, N. (1991). *Pish, Posh, Said Hieronymus Bosch*. New York: Harcourt Brace.

Willems, M. (2004). *Don't Let the Pigeon Drive the Bus*. New York: Hyperion.

Williams, S. (1997). *Library Lil*. New York: Scholastic.

Wood, A. (1996). *Bright and Early Thursday Evening: A Tangled Tale*. New York: Harcourt Brace.

Wood, A. (1996). *The Bunyans*. New York: Scholastic.

# Index